TEMARI *Techniques*

A Visual Guide to Making Japanese Embroidered Thread Balls

Barbara B. Suess

Breckling Press

Library of Congress Cataloging-in-Publication Data

Suess, Barbara B.
  Temari techniques : a visual guide to making Japanese embroidered thread
balls / Barbara B. Suess
    pages cm
  Includes bibliographical references and index.
  ISBN 978-1-933308-32-6
1. Fancy work--Japan. 2. Embroidery--Japan. 3. Decorative balls--Japan.
I. Title.

TT751.S945 2007

746.44--dc23

                        2012001923

Editorial and art direction by Anne Knudsen
Cover and interior design by Maria Mann
Cover and interior photographs by Sharon Hoogstraten
Technical drawings by Barbara B. Suess
This book was set in Bembo, Neutra, Hiroshige

Published by Breckling Press
283 N. Michigan St, Elmhurst, IL 60126

Printed and bound in China

International Standard Book Number: 978-1-933308-32-6

Dedication

Temari Techniques is for the mothers, grandmothers, and fiber artists of Japan who have created temari through the centuries, especially Chiyoko Ozaki and Toshiko Ozaki (mother and daughter) who dedicated their lives to temari.

The book is also dedicated to the many stitchers who have generously shared their time and thoughts as we worked to learn even the most basic techniques without formal instruction.

From the collection of Barbara Suess

Contents

About This Book 1

CHAPTER 1 The Allure of an Ancient Craft
Origins of Temari 5
Popularity of Temari 6
Language of Temari 7

CHAPTER 2 Materials
Temari Tools 12
Threads 13

CHAPTER 3 Making the Core
Creating the Core 17
Wrapping the Core 19

CHAPTER 4 Adding Guidelines
Using a Paper Measuring Strip 25
Thread Skills 27
Making Guidelines:
    Standard Temari Divisions 29
Simple Divisions 31
Combination Divisions 33
Using Temari Diagrams 42
Adding Support Guidelines 46
Marking Multi-Centers (Subdividing C10) 53

CHAPTER 5 Simple Stitching and Wrapping Techniques
Surface Embroidery Stitches 57
    Mums Pattern 61
    Pine Shapes Pattern 63
    Caribbean Swirls Pattern 67
Wrapping 67
    Bermuda Reef Pattern 70
    Blueberry Pie Pattern 72
    Nautical Mosaic Pattern 73
    Summer Picnic Basket Pattern 77
    Little Quilt Square Pattern 77

CHAPTER 6 Stitching Simple Shapes
Open Shapes 79
    Square Dance Pattern 83
Solid Shapes 84
    Daffodil Pattern 86
Spindles 87
    Lemon Slices Pattern 88
Intersecting Shapes 89
    Pinwheel Pattern 90
    Evening Star Pattern 93

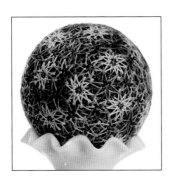  

CHAPTER 7 **Herringbone Stitches**

Herringbone and Double Herringbone 95
Net Stitching 97
   Forest Flower Pattern 98
Kiku Herringbone 99
   Clematis Bloom Pattern 101
   Dusty Rose Pattern 101
Reverse Kiku Herringbone 102
   Classic Kiku Pattern 104
   Red Dahlia Pattern 104
Ribbed Kiku Herringbone 105
Descending Herringbone 106
   Jasmine Pattern 107

CHAPTER 8 **More Stitching Techniques**

Merry-Go-Round Stitching 109
   Merry-Go-Round with
    Kiku Herringbone Pattern 114
Continuous Motifs 115
   Pearl Star Pattern 118
   Mariposa Lily Pattern 119
   Whirly Bird Pattern 121
   Hot Pink Star Pattern 123
   Classic Hito Hude Gake Pattern 127
Continuous Paths Stitching 129
   Diamond Dance Pattern 129

CHAPTER 9 **Challenge Designs**

Rose Design 133
   Raulston Roses Pattern 134
Mitsubishi and Other Diamond Designs 135
   Three Diamonds Pattern 137
   Four Diamonds Pattern 138
   Five Diamonds Pattern 138
Weaving Techniques to Fill Shapes 139
   Weave Study Pattern 142
   Woven Bamboo Pattern 143
Flax Leaf 145
   Country Night Pattern 146
   Filigree Flax Pattern 148
More Challenge Designs 151
   Interlocked Puzzle Pattern 152
   Emerald Isle Pattern 154
   Asters Pattern 156

CHAPTER 10 **Design and Display**

Elements of Temari Design 157
   Abstracted Stars Pattern 167
   Four Tops Pattern 167
   Buttercups Pattern 169
Temari Display 171

APPENDICES

Index 197

Acknowledgements

From the collection of Barbara Suess

Abundant thanks: To Debi Abolt for her significant contributions to this book including but not limited to the organization of hundreds of tiny details that make up the art of temari and her much valued feedback on all aspects of temari making; To pattern testers and editors Jannett, Rebecca, Rosemary, Laura, Jane, Janis, Jean, Jeanne, Martha, Pat, Carol S., Katherine, Dana, Margaret, and Carol W. To translators Ai, Hiro, Janet, Junji, Kei, Mari, and Misako; Special thanks to Dana Watson who generously gave her time to proofread the entire book. To Kathy Hewitt for her encouragement and support;

To these companies for their generosity and help in selecting beautiful thread for temari: Caron, Coats and Clark, DMC, Kreinik, Rainbow Gallery, and Vineyard Silk. Read more about these companies in the Sources section (page 178);

To Anne Knudsen at Breckling Press; Last but not least, to family and close friends who allowed space and time for many months of hard work.

A Message from Barb

A few years ago, a good friend told me that, in her family, talent with the needle always skipped a generation. Thank goodness that's not the case in my family. Mama and I both love stitching. While in college, crochet and knitting were hobbies I squeezed in between studies in landscape design. Later, when my first daughter was born, Mama taught me English smocking and shared patterns for fancy dresses dripping with French lace. I made so many dresses that my little girl could never have worn them all. So every few months, I would have to hold a sale in my home to clear out so I could have room to continue!

Hand embroidery and quilting remain my favorite activities for expressing my creative side. Living in Yokohama, Japan, for four years in the late 1980s had a profound and lasting effect on me. When I discovered embroidered Japanese temari in 2000, I knew I'd found *the* needlecraft for me. The symmetry of design and deep symbolism of temari touch my heart.

Each temari is a different combination of design elements, a puzzle to figure out and put together with thread. Wrapping the ball with yarn and thread then stitching repetitive patterns is a soothing, meditative activity for me. I like to begin with an idea that I want to express—the simplicity of a spring flower, a cool night in the Appalachian Mountains, or a Celtic knot made of interlocking geometrical shapes. Then I dive into boxes of threads to choose colors and textures. I stitch it out, give it a name, snap a photo and find a home for my newest temari.

It's my hope that new and experienced temari makers will use this book to learn the techniques and be inspired by the designs to create their own small works of art. We can then keep this ever-fascinating craft alive and strong. In a newsletter from the Japan Temari Association, Sensei Ozaki expressed her desire to see the art of temari spread through the world, thereby extending the *wa*, the circle of harmony, peace, and balance. Let's do just that.

About This Book

Temari Techniques is designed to be a source of knowledge and inspiration for temari artists at all experience levels. There are many different ways to make a temari. You'll find lots of options given here, so take time to familiarize yourself with the book then experiment to choose your favorite techniques.

Getting Started

If you are a beginner, start by reading the introductory material to learn how to make a temari and how to add guidelines to mark a simple division. Then jump to Chapter 5 where you will find lessons on some of the basic stitches and simple projects for practice. After you become familiar with making the ball and marking simple divisions, come back to Chapter 4, Adding Guidelines, and learn how to make more complicated combination divisions.

If you are an intermediate stitcher, you can jump right in to any part of the book, using it as a reference. Take the time to stitch some projects that you may have missed in your previous exploration of the craft. Practice the introductory techniques until they become second nature, concentrating on all those little skills that add up to make your stitching crisp and precise. Experienced stitchers can find help by looking for tips labeled "Refine Your Skills."

If you are an advanced stitcher, use the details in the marking and stitching sections to refine and expand your techniques. Read about the different ways to mark multi-center divisions (see page 53). Check out the Challenge Designs in Chapter 9; the material here will help you make your own creations by putting the stitches together in new ways.

Opposite: Summer Picnic Basket, see page 77

Stitches and Designs

Types of stitches and designs are grouped by similarity of execution and arranged in order of difficulty. Each technique is explained with step-by-step directions, followed by a pattern for a small project to help you learn and practice that particular technique. While these patterns may seem basic to an experienced temari stitcher, keep in mind that they are designed to help the stitcher focus on a single technique, either for initial learning or for technique mastery.

The patterns in Chapter 9 are written to challenge and inspire. They range from intermediate to advanced designs and are explained in greater detail, combining ideas and techniques that are taught earlier in the book. Each design has references to the techniques used so you can read up on them before you start.

Temari Terms

In choosing words to describe temari techniques, stitches, and patterns, I felt it was important to honor the traditions of temari makers in Japan who have been stitching for hundreds of years. In most cases, the English name used for the term comes directly from a translation of the Japanese name. For instance, *masu kagari* means "square stitching" and *kousa kagari* means "layered stitching." In some cases, the direct Japanese translation is too long or too awkward to be used as the English name. For instance, this is the case with *mitsubane kikkou kagari*, which is translated as "three wings or feathers arranged like on the end of an arrow and tortoise shell stitching." I shortened this one to "tri-wing stitching." In this book, you will find both the English and the Japanese names for each technique, hopefully avoiding any confusion.

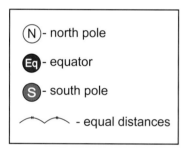

These simple diagram symbols help you keep track of where you are

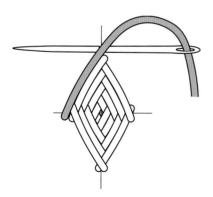

In the drawings, the working thread is always shown in color and the previous stitching is shown in white

Finding Your Way Around the Book

You will find a complete illustrated list of temari divisions and stitches in the Visual Reference on pages 181–192. Use these pages to quickly find instructions for temari techniques in the book when you don't know the name of the division or stitch.

Solid and Dashed Lines

Division lines are solid when they denote simple divisions or combination divisions. Extra support lines added for special designs are shown as dashed lines in the diagrams and are usually made with the same guideline thread.

Measuring

Most measuring for temari is done with a narrow strip of paper, cut to fit your ball, and folded to divide it into equal sections (see Chapter 4). Simple! Other measurements are made with a narrow tape measure using centimeters and the metric system. Even though all measurements are given both in centimeters and inches, make it easy on yourself by using metric. For example, when dividing the equator length into sections, it is much easier to divide 24 cm into sections than it is to divide 9¾".

Pattern directions often place the first stitch of a row by referring to a fraction of the distance between the pole and the equator. Using this relational method rather than giving a set measurement (such as 1 cm) gives you the ability to easily transfer the pattern to smaller or larger temari without much distortion of the design.

Index

Use the index on pages 197–199 for cross referencing various techniques and designs to locate the directions in the book.

Measure by Eye

From the very beginning, try to train your eye to judge distances. When you want to divide a line into four sections, first use your eye to determine the half-way point, then place a stitch there. Again by eye, find the half-way points on both these sections of the original line and place a stitch at each. You have split the original length into four sections. For most temari designs, you will find this type of measuring is entirely sufficient. With an experienced eye, you will learn to look at the entire temari and spot when your stitching might be going slightly astray, making corrections as you work to even up the design.

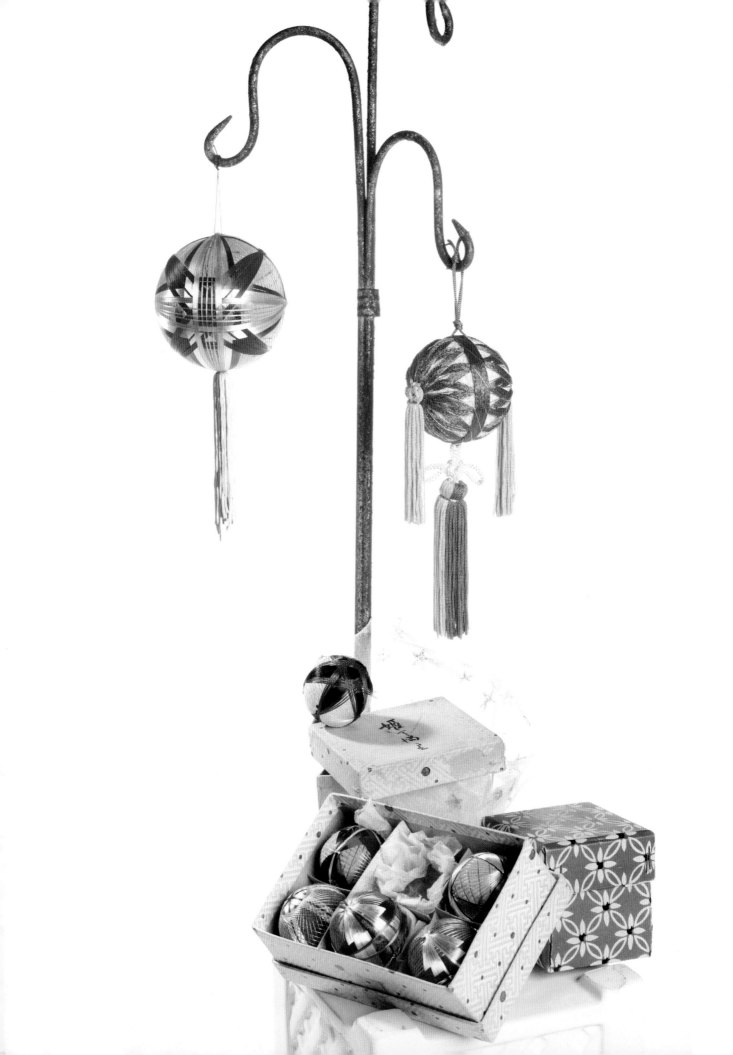

Allure of an Ancient Craft

When you look at a beautiful quilt, it is easy to see how the craft could have started with a mother carefully reusing old fabric scraps to make a pretty and useful blanket for her family. A needlework sampler or embroidered picture brings to mind the idea of ladies seeking ways to embellish clothing or linens. However, when you look at a beautifully displayed modern temari, it's more difficult to imagine just how this unusual craft could have begun and evolved. Although now hundreds of years old and far removed from its initial purposes, Japanese temari remains a craft based on recycling, artistic expression, and heartfelt giving.

Origins of Temari

Temari is thought to have its origin in *kemari*, a game played with a deerskin ball. This kickball game was introduced to Japan from China during the Asuka Period (538-710), along with many significant artistic, social, political, and religious ideas, such as Buddhism. Later *onna-mari* (literally translated as lady-ball) were made from silk threads by palace maidservants in competitions to please their princesses. The games ladies played with temari involved sitting on the floor and rolling the balls between them.

Opposite and this page: Vintage temari from the collection of Barbara Suess

Here and opposite: vintage postcards from the collection of Barbara Suess

When cotton manufacturing became prevalent in Japan during the Edo Period (1600-1868), temari making moved from the upper classes to the common people. The use of this affordable fiber allowed the craft to spread throughout the country, with artists from each area developing new designs by using the materials and colors available to them. Children used temari to play tossing and juggling games. Rhythmic *temari uta*, songs and chants like those sung by Western children while skipping rope, began to accompany the games.

In the early 1900s, the rubber ball replaced homemade temari as a popular toy and the craft dwindled. However, temari remained popular gift items. New Year's Day, *Hinamatsuri* (Japanese Doll Festival), the birth of a child, and weddings were special occasions that called for the creation of a new temari. The craft evolved from making homemade toys to creating small works of art. Temari are still given as gifts today and are more often displayed within the home rather than used as toys.

Popularity of Temari

The publication of the first instructional book on temari, *Temari Juni Kagetsu* or *Twelve Months of Temari* by Chiyoko Ozaki in 1968 was a milestone in documenting the craft's history and designs. Before that, temari traditions had been passed through generations of women from as far back as the Muromachi Period (1366-1573).

In the years following the release of Ozaki's first book, many more temari books have been published in Japan, especially in the last fifteen years. Each of these books is a delight, filled with colorful photographs and intricate diagrams useful to the avid temari stitcher. Some are the works of a particular artist or group; others are based on themes symbolizing values from Japanese culture. Flowers, birds, animals, and everyday objects represent love, long life, abundance, courage, and other blessings. Geometric designs, ranging from simple to intricate, display how unique each temari can be with a simple change of color or base division.

In 1979, the Japan Temari Association (Temari no Kai) was established and headquartered in Tokyo. Its purpose is "to pass on the art and tradition of Japanese temari, to heighten its artistry, and to educate the successors of temari-making." Another major goal is "to deepen the understanding among members as well as to aid in cultural exchange with other nations and to help improve Japanese culture." The JTA promotes learning through a technique examination, where members can apply for certification at four different levels. The organization hosts a public gallery; holds classes, seminars and meetings; arranges cultural exchanges with foreign countries; and publishes books and newsletters on a regular basis.

Language of Temari

During the last five to ten years, there has been phenomenal growth in the number of temari stitchers outside Japan. This is mainly due to the ease of communication facilitated by the internet and an increased number of English language temari publications. Temari artists scattered

Furosato no Temari

The book *Furosato no Temari or Hometown Temari* by Tomokazu Arai was published in Japanese in 1990. The author traveled across the country and interviewed temari makers to document how they learned the craft as well as their techniques and designs. *Furosato no Temari* is filled with photographs of temari and the stories behind them. Most interesting to a temari artist today are all the different methods for making the core. The ingredients are mostly all-natural and taken from what is abundant around the residence of the artist.

A traditional way to make the core in Tsuruoka City was to take a clamshell, fill it with sand, pack wood chips around it, then wrap it again with *zenmai* (fern fibers), and complete by wrapping the core with thread.

In the old days of Matsumoto, people went into the mountains and collected cocoons to use as cores. They would roll fern fibers around the core, then stitch the design with thread dyed with plant extracts such as indigo. In many cases, the stitching was only the last, small part of the whole process.

A temari maker from Muraoka used grass seeds for the core to make her temari hard enough to bounce.

In Shuugetsu temari, a seashell with a small stone in it was used as the core, then wrapped with rice husks. This temari made a very light sound when shaken.

Temari makers from many areas used the dried fibers of a sago palm as the core filling, cotton clothing, and thread scraps for wrapping around the core, and recycled thread for stitching a design.

The largest temari were called *kinsuke mari*, and they reached sizes up to two feet in diameter. The core was made of wooden shavings rolled up with threads and covered with a cloth. Next, an artist was employed to make a rough drawing on the cloth and embroidery was added directly over the drawing.

From its very beginning, temari has exemplified a mother's love for her child. In many regions, temari are handed down from generation to generation. The one thing all temari have in common is that they were made by mothers to show love for their children. Mrs. Nori Furuta said, "Every time I hold these temari my mother left for me, I remember my mother. They make me happy but a little sad at the same time since I feel that my mother is still talking to me."

Hundreds of years ago, temari evolved as a craft of recycling, as Japanese mothers used kimono scraps to make toys for their children. Feel free to transform leftovers from your other fiber arts and crafts into these small works of art. Make use of bits of batting, fabric, and yarn for the core. Throughout the book, temari are stitched with a variety of threads to show off many possibilities. Pattern directions give color names so you can substitute from your stash. Explore with color! Experiment with texture!

around the world no longer feel isolated or that they have to "reinvent the wheel" each time they begin a new design. Communication, often instant due to the internet, has allowed the sharing of temari techniques to foster a quick growth of skills for individual artists.

With so much of our communication shared through the written word, developing a common temari language has been essential for our technical and artistic growth. Without words we all understand, skills developed through trial and error cannot be easily communicated to other artists. Stagnation in learning and creativity occurs when we can't meaningfully share our individual discoveries. Of course, there is common temari terminology—in Japanese! Non-Japanese enthusiasts have found the need to develop an English equivalent for common Japanese terms. Even the ability to precisely describe simple concepts, such as the placement of a stitch on a particular thread guideline, makes written patterns easier to understand and more accurate. When we learned to recognize temari stitches by translated English names, we made them our own and became comfortable designing with them. Each new discovery in Japanese needed corresponding English terminology. The English language of temari is still evolving. As the years go by, some terms may win out over others by more common usage. In the long run, it doesn't matter which terms we use as long as we can understand one another.

Temari enthusiasts are attracted to this unique craft for many different reasons—the colors, designs, symmetry, or simply the allure of an ancient craft. Feeling a connection to the past while pulling a threaded needle through the ball can be just as meaningful as discovering a brand new design. This is one time when past, present, and future go hand-in-hand. That's the beauty of temari.

Temari Tools and Materials

A small basket or box will hold the few tools and threads that you need for stitching temari. Keep them together one place so your project is easily portable when you want to take your embroidery along with you. Remembering that temari are traditionally made from recycled materials. Keep your eyes open for ingredients you can use for your temari cores. Become an avid collector of colorful stitching threads! You will be amazed how quickly your collection grows.

Temari Tools

The tools needed for temari stitching are much the same as those used for other kinds of needlework. You probably already own most of them; if not, you can find them in your local sewing, needlework, or craft store. You will need:

- Pins with colored tops and a pin cushion: 1 ¼" to 1 ½" long pins in a variety of colors. These are used for marking the ball and for keeping your place while stitching.

- Needles: a long (2" or more) sharp needle with an eye large enough for perle cotton. A darner needle, size 18 or longer, is a good choice. Consider a short, blunt tipped needle (#18 tapestry) for projects where you will be doing lots of weaving and little actual stitching.

- Small, sharp scissors: for cutting thread and paper.

- Paper measuring strip: used for marking the temari. It should be about ¼" to ³/₈" wide and long enough to go around your ball. You can cut this yourself from regular paper or use paper quilling strips. For larger temari, tape two strips together end-to-end. (See page 25.)

It's fairly easy to thread a temari
needle because it has such a
large eye. However if you have
trouble, try cutting a small strip
of paper, no wider than the eye
of the needle and less than 2"
long. Fold the paper in half over
the end of the troublesome
thread. Push the folded end
of the paper with the thread
through the eye of your needle.

- Tape measure: narrow (about $^3/_8$" wide), cloth or plastic, and marked with both centimeters and inches. A retractable tape measure is handy.

- Paper circle guide (optional): use a stencil or your computer's illustration or word processing program to create circles of various sizes. Pin one to an intersection of threads and use the edge of the circle as a guide for stitching the first row of a design. You could use buttons of various sizes for this as well. See Appendix for circle guides to copy.

- V-ruler (optional): a specialty measuring device that is useful in a variety of ways. This small, plastic, "V" shaped ruler was designed specifically for marking a combination 10 division (C10), but it can be used whenever you need to measure short distances on the ball. This is one item you'll have to order from someone who specializes in temari supplies. (See photograph on page 41.)

- Thimble (optional): to protect your finger during long stitching sessions. Not everyone chooses to use one, but you may find you like added protection from the large needle.

- Pillow (optional): to support your temari as you stitch. It can be difficult to hold the ball while stitching. A small pillow placed on your lap is the perfect solution.

Threads

Threads are used for wrapping and marking the ball as well as stitching the design. Regular sewing machine thread is the best fiber for wrapping the outer thread layer. Take care to match its color to your design's color scheme because it will become your stitching surface. Serger or overlock thread that comes on large cones is an economical choice. You should avoid slick or shiny threads, as they tend to slip off the ball when you try to wrap with them.

Guideline threads are used to mark the ball into sections; they are often glitzy metallic threads, but other choices work as well. Look for one that is the same size or slightly smaller than your design thread. Generally, more intricate marking requires finer thread. Sometimes the guidelines are an integral part of the finished design, but other times you will want them to be less noticeable. For inconspicuous guidelines, try using fine perle cotton (sizes #8 or #12) in a color that matches your wrapping thread. Alternatively, you can mark with a fine perle cotton or sewing thread in a contrasting color and then remove the guidelines after stitching the design.

Your choice for design threads is almost limitless! Twisted fibers such as perle cotton that do not need to be separated into strands are the easiest to use. The most commonly used size is #5 perle cotton. Size #8 perle cotton is a nice alternative when you need a finer thread for a more detailed design. Experiment with variegated, hand dyed, and overdyed threads—each can be a beautiful part of your design.

Stranded threads such as embroidery floss also work well for temari, but they require a bit more patience and therefore are not typically recommended for beginners. Whether you choose to separate the strands and lay them flat with each stitch or to use them twisted together as they come off the skein, you'll need to adjust them as you stitch to maintain a consistent appearance on the ball.

Refine Your Skills Matching Thread Size to the Design

The size of threads you use to mark and stitch your temari can make a big difference to the success of the design. The size of the ball, complexity of the design, and size of the stitching threads are all related. In general, the smaller the ball or the more complex the design, the finer your stitching thread should be. Keep this in mind when you are stitching on a different size ball than the one called for in a pattern or when you are designing your own patterns. If you choose a thread that is too large, you'll find that you can't fit the correct number of rows into the allotted space. Choose a thread that's too small and you may find that you have to keep stitching forever to fill up a space.

Experiment with different thread sizes and spacing until you get the perfect fit.

Choosing Design Threads for Texture

Your choice of stitching thread can add much more than color to your designs. Thread today is available in a large variety of fibers and textures that can enhance the way the finished temari looks on display and the way it feels in your hands. Silk and rayon are good choices for a beautiful shine. Look for cotton velvet threads to add rich texture and depth of color. Wool or linen fibers have a rough look that might be just what you need as a contrast to a smoother fiber. Wispy or fuzzy fibers can bring a whimsical look to the ball, or they can provide just the sparkle you need for a wintry, snowflake design.

When you combine different textures of thread on the same design, you bring an extra dimension to the temari. For most designs, it's helpful to keep to threads that are similar in size. If you do choose to use different sized threads on the same ball, you may need to change the number of rows for each thread so the design works out as planned. Each type of fiber will have its own special characteristics, so if you are stitching with the thread for the first time, allow a little extra time and thread for experimenting.

A pin cushion in a tea cup!

Making the Core

There are many different ways to make a temari ball. It seems everyone eventually settles on the method that suits them best, using materials readily available to them. This chapter will show you how to create and wrap a perfect core for your ball. Not only must it look beautiful and be evenly wrapped, it must be firm to the touch yet soft enough to use as a stitching surface. In addition, it must roll smoothly and be made for easy and comfortable stitching.

Creating the Core

Begin by selecting materials for the center of the ball (these will be invisible under the thread and yarn wrap you will add later). First you'll need a container of some sort—socks are ideal. Maybe it's time to clean out your sock drawer or use those lonely, orphaned dryer socks for a higher purpose. Other container options are a stocking cut off at the ankle or a thin plastic bag (cut off the top if it is a zip lock). One pair of panty hose can go a long way. Cut a section 6" to 8" long and stitch one end closed with sewing thread to get it ready for filling.

The filling should be soft and easy to mold into the shape of a ball. Some good choices are dryer lint, old socks without heavy elastic, thread and yarn orts (left-over bits), or small scraps of fabric and batting. A core made with just batting is too soft; a core made completely from fabric is too hard. A combination of the two is just right.

Opposite: Desert Spirit. See also page 48

Japanese Filler

In Japan, rice hulls are a traditional filling and they have become a favorite for many temari makers worldwide. You can find rice hulls at wine and beer home-brewing stores, where they are usually sold by the pound to be used as a filtering medium for the brew. When you use one cup of hulls per core, one pound of rice hulls will yield about sixteen temari.

Adding dried lavender leaves, other herbs, or scented oils in the core makes a very special temari. Just be sure that the filling is clean, dry, and free of insects and mold. Scented oils should be placed deep inside the ball so there is no possibility that they will seep through the layers and come in contact with the stitching on the ball's surface.

After filling your container with selected materials, neatly fold over the open end. There is no need to sew it shut as the first few wraps of yarn will keep it closed.

Add a Bell Box

Delightful sounds come from a temari with a bell box in the center! Make a tiny box of cardstock and fill it with jingle bells, beads, rice, small stones, or shells. You can also use two bottle caps taped together as a container. If you are planning to give the temari as a gift, consider the recipient when selecting items to enclose in the core. Write a wish or prayer on a small slip of paper and tuck it into the core. Choose small, meaningful items to put in the core so the temari is beautiful inside and out.

Refine Your Skills Bin Temari or Temari in a Bottle

A curiosity much like a ship in a bottle, *bin temari* are popular in Japan. What's the secret? Construct your temari ball with a core that can be removed, collapse the stitched ball, slip it into the bottle, and re-stuff the core with cotton or batting through the opening of the bottle. First measure the opening of your bottle. Loosely wind a thick, slippery cord (nylon or polyester) into a ball that measures slightly smaller than the bottle opening and place it in a thin plastic bag. Wrap the bag with yarn and thread, leaving the end of the cord and the opening edge of the plastic bag sticking out of the thread wrap. Choose a temari design with small stitches that cover the ball completely and will hold the ball together when you remove the cord. Slowly pull the cord out of the temari core and slip the ball into the container. Using a chop stick, stuff batting into the plastic bag in the core until the ball is back to its original size. Carefully rearrange the yarn and thread wrap to cover the hole.

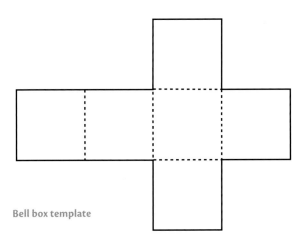

Bell box template

Warning: it can be very frustrating when your guide pins hit the bell box and won't stay in the correct place. If you are attempting a division or pattern that is new to you, make the box very small and make sure it is buried deep in the center of the core or simply leave it out entirely.

To make a bell box, use the pattern shown here and follow these steps.

1 Trace the pattern onto cardstock; a recycled greeting card is fine.

2 Fold along the dotted lines.

3 Tape the sides together and fill the box with your selected items.

4 Tape the lid shut.

Wrapping the Core

The tension you use when wrapping the ball can make a big difference in the final feel of your temari. Ideally, you want a ball that is firm enough to hold its shape yet soft enough to stitch through comfortably. Relax while wrapping. Make sure not to think about the stresses in your life, or your temari will turn out as solid as a rock!

Use different levels of tension when making a ball, beginning with a loose yarn wrap and ending with a snug thread wrap.

• Very light tension: used for wrapping yarn around the core. As the yarn flows through your hand, guide it onto the ball while barely touching it.

• Medium tension: used for power wrapping the thread layer. Let the threads flow through your hand, touching all of your curled fingers while applying very light pressure on the thread with your thumb.

Using a Firm Core

If you decide to use a Styrofoam® ball as the core instead of using a compressible filling, pay extra attention to the yarn wrapping stage to make sure that the yarn is distributed evenly over the ball and is not wrapped too tightly. If you find a bump while wrapping with thread, press it down, slightly crushing the Styrofoam. It's a bit more difficult to create a very round ball when using such a firm center. However, Styrofoam is excellent for making hanging ornaments due to its light weight.

- Snug tension: used for the last, single-strand layer of the thread wrap. Let the thread flow through your hand as with medium tension, but pull on the thread a bit to increase the tension. If you are making dents in the ball, that's too much pressure.

Using these different levels of tension will help you create a round ball with a snugly wrapped outer surface to securely hold your stitches and an under layer of yarn through which your needle can easily pass. You should never have to use pliers to pull the needle through the ball!

Wrap with Yarn

Soft baby yarn is best for temari. The thickness and number of plies doesn't really matter as long as the yarn compresses a lot when squeezed. To recycle coarse yarn into temari, use it first when wrapping the core, then add a layer of softer yarn on top. You can use any color since this yarn layer will be totally covered by thread in the next step. Using contrasting colors for yarn and thread helps you see when the yarn layer is totally covered and will help ensure that you get a thick enough thread wrap.

Refine Your Skills Adjust the Firmness of Your Ball for the Design

Every temari maker ends up with their own preferred feel for their temari. As long as you can stitch on it accurately and without difficulty, it is your choice how hard or soft to make the ball. However, if you are someone who naturally makes a softer ball, you may find that for some designs a firmer ball with a tighter thread wrap is necessary. In general, if the design has most of the stitching in a single direction, like a wrapped design or a merry-go-round design, you will want a firmer ball so that the pressure from the stitching does not compress the temari out of shape. Intricate designs with many precisely placed stitches,

like a swirl or flax filled shape, benefit from a tighter and thicker thread wrap to help you keep the stitches placed exactly where you want them. This is another instance where experience will be an excellent teacher. If your finished temari seems misshapen or your stitches don't seem to stay right where you placed them, the culprit could be that your ball is too soft or your thread wrap is not tight enough. Sometimes just a little more tension in the thread wrap is all that is needed to fix the problem. Once you learn what sorts of designs require a change from your normal method, you can plan ahead when you wrap.

Wrap this first layer with very light, even tension. Wrap randomly by turning the ball constantly. Wrap and turn the ball, wrap and turn the ball, all in one smooth motion. When you see an area where several layers of yarn are piled up and a bump has formed, avoid wrapping over this spot for the next few turns of the ball. Stop two or three times to gently roll the temari around in the palms of your hands with the goal of making it round. See a bump? Gently press it down and continue wrapping.

When you are wrapping yarn or thread on the ball, always wrap across the center or fattest part of the ball, not off to one edge. The yarn or thread will not slip off the ball when it's away from the edge.

Our tendency is to wrap in parallel rows around the ball—not a good thing for temari. Your ball will end up shaped like a pumpkin instead of a round globe. You may have to force yourself to keep your eye on the ball and turn it constantly until wrapping randomly becomes natural.

Look carefully at the yarn-wrapped ball when you are done. You should have a round ball and the outer layer should be randomly wrapped, so that you can't see any single yarn strands piled up in one place.

Care and Cleaning

Finding vintage temari in Japan is not an easy task. In the old days, temari were used as toys by children and this play distressed the fibers so they discolored or broke. You can find exquisite balls from the mid-twentieth century that were obviously not used for play but were put on display and handled gently. Colors may have faded since many temari were stitched using threads treated with natural dyes.

Today we can create temari to last a lifetime or more by using strong perle cotton or silk threads for stitching. Choose a metallic thread with care since sometimes it will split and break if not twisted tightly. Anchor all threads securely into the thread wrapped ball.

Caring for your finished temari is as simple as removing the dust now and then if they are displayed in an open room. Wipe each ball off with a dry rag or blow it with a can of compressed air. When the core is made with rice hulls, the shape can be distorted out of round if balls are stored in a bin or bowl with others. You can mold these back into shape by gently rolling and compressing the ball with the palms of your hands. Very intricately stitched temari deserve a place behind glass in a display cabinet, perhaps under lights, where they will receive little handling and need very little care.

Now, measure the ball. Your temari should be about 1 cm (3/8") smaller than this after you've wrapped it with thread in the next step. The thread wrap compresses the ball a bit since it is wrapped with more tension than the yarn wrap. You can make the ball larger at this point by adding more yarn.

Next, Wrap with Thread

Wrap regular sewing machine or serger thread over the yarn layer. To quickly cover the yarn and create a strong thread base to hold your stitches, wrap with several strands of thread at once. This is called power wrapping. It will fill in the gaps between large strands of yarn and give a smoother surface for the final thread wrap. Three strands is the minimum for power wrapping; five or six are even better. These threads do not need to be all the same color but it will make the final thread wrap quicker if they are.

Gather up the ends of the thread and wrap the ball with all of the threads at once, holding it directly above the cones of thread. Just like when you were wrapping with yarn, be sure to turn the ball constantly and wrap randomly so you don't have thread piling up in one spot. Wrap with medium tension. Remember that you want to be able to pass a needle easily through this layer when you are ready to stitch, so don't wrap too tightly.

When the yarn layer is totally covered and the surface of the ball feels rather smooth, clip off all but one of the threads. This thread will be your final wrap color. Start a new thread of a different color if you did not use the same color for power wrapping. Continue wrapping this final outer layer until you have a fine finish on the ball and the power wrapped layer is totally covered. Use the same proper wrapping techniques as before:

Teenie Temari

Miniature temari make adorable beads, earrings, and key chain fobs. Begin with about half a tissue and roll it into a ball. Power wrap with several strands of thread in your selected background color. Finish wrapping with a single strand of thread. You probably won't be able to measure the teenie to apply guidelines so just eyeball the distances and place guide pins in the ball for the pole and equator. Mark and stitch with #8 perle cotton (or finer) thread.

turn the ball constantly and wrap randomly with even tension. Tighten up on the tension a bit towards the end. This top layer will hold your stitching so that it doesn't pull out of its proper place on the ball.

End off by cutting the thread from the spool with a tail about 24" long. Thread this tail through a needle and stitch in a zigzag path over the ball's surface, placing the stitches a couple of inches apart. When you come to the end of your stitching thread, cut the thread even with the ball's surface.

Fix Loose Thread Wrap

Is your thread wrap too loose? This can easily happen. Hopefully, if your final layer of thread wrap was snug and your final stitches were placed securely, the thread wrap will not come loose. Guidelines and stitching threads will also help hold the thread wrap in place. But if it does come loose, you will need to tuck the loose thread back into the thread wrap. If it is a long length of thread, use your needle. Pass a loop of the loose thread through the needle's eye and take a stitch under the ball's surface to hide the thread. Shorter loose lengths can be pushed down under the thread wrap with the eye end of your needle or another blunt-tipped tool.

Next time, try to wrap the outer layer tighter and right across the middle of the ball.

Adding Guidelines

Temari designs seem to float on the ball in a beautifully organized, often symmetrical fashion. The secret is a system of guidelines that you put in place using a surprisingly easy method. Before going into detail on stitching the guidelines, there are a few techniques you need to learn. One is using a simple tool that will ensure accuracy as you work—a paper measuring strip. Another is effectively using pins to help you place the guidelines. You will then turn to working with thread; that is, learning how to start and stop stitching so that your finished ball is as perfect as it can be.

Using a Paper Measuring Strip

Since the balls you wrap vary in size, you will need to make a new paper measuring strip for every temari ball you create. Use it to place guide pins for the north pole, south pole, and equator.

1   Start by cutting a strip of paper about ¼" wide and a bit longer than the distance around the ball. Don't worry if the strip is too long—you can cut off any extra length later. If your temari is too large for a normal paper strip, tape two strips together or cut your strips from a legal size sheet of paper. Fold back one end of the strip about ¼" and pin it to the ball through the crease mark. This will be your north pole.

Opposite: Classic Hito Hude Gake (lower left). The pattern is on page 127. For a more intricate design, add more guidelines: 32 centers (lower right) and 92 centers (top)

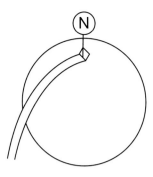

Step 1 Place north pole pin

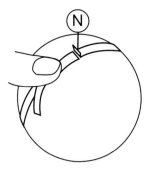

Step 2 Fit paper strip to ball

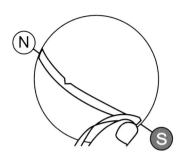

Step 4 Place south pole pin

2   Wrap the strip around the ball, making sure the fit is snug. Fold the end back so that the fold rests against the shaft of the pin. Double check for accuracy by releasing the free end, pivoting the strip a quarter turn around the ball, and measuring again. Refold if necessary, then cut along the fold.

3   With the strip still pinned to the ball, fold it in half by bringing the cut end up to the shaft of the pin, then crease the strip to mark the halfway point. This will be used to place your south pole pin. Cut a small, shallow notch off the corner of the creased edge. Fold in half again and crease once more. Cut a small notch to use for placing guide pins at the equator.

4   Mark the south pole by opening the paper strip completely, then refolding it in half. Lay it smoothly around the ball and stick a pin straight down next to the center fold to mark the south pole. Recheck

Paper Strip Troubleshooting

If your strip fits when you measure it one way, but doesn't fit another way, check your ball and make sure it is completely round. Roll it in the palms of your hands to smooth out any bumps. If the thread wrap becomes loose, add another thin layer until you are sure it is snugly wrapped, then test your paper strip again. Often you can mold a ball this way, measure again, and find out that your paper strip fits in all directions.

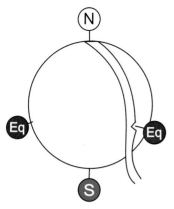

Step 4 Place equator pins

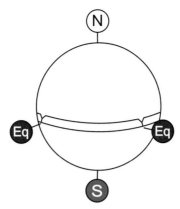

Step 5 Check for equidistance

the pin's position several times by pivoting the paper strip at the north pole pin. Next, use the crease mark you made a quarter of the way along the strip to mark the equator. The number of equator pins you place is determined by which division you are making (see Simple Divisions, page 31). Be sure to use the crease marks (not the notches) for pin placement.

5   Carefully remove the paper strip from the ball by snipping it free from the north pole pin. Wrap the paper strip around the equator and use the crease marks to check that the equator pins are equidistant. Shift the pins sideways as needed to accurately divide the equator into the number of divisions for your design. Keep the strip with your ball until the design is complete. You can use it for measuring thread lengths for wraps or as a quick reference when placing stitches.

Thread Skills

Mastering some basic thread skills will make your temari stitching more successful and enjoyable. Unlike conventional sewing, with temari there is no "wrong side" so there is nowhere to hide knots—or mistakes!

Starting Your Thread

Whether you are adding guidelines or beginning stitching, there are two techniques for starting your thread. One involves leaving the thread attached to the spool. The other starts with a cut length of thread.

Starting with the thread attached to the spool can be a timesaver when wrapping guidelines or making wrapped bands, since then you won't have to measure or estimate thread length. Begin by threading a needle with the loose end of a spool, card, or skein of thread. Insert

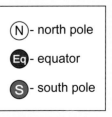

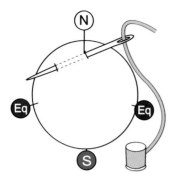

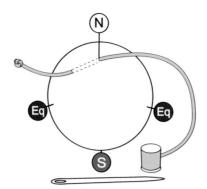

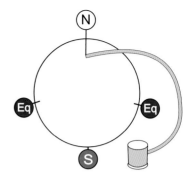

Start with thread on spool: enter at north pole and exit 2" away

Remove needle and make knot

Tug on thread to bury knot

the needle at the starting point (which is always the north pole when wrapping guidelines) and exit 2" away. Remove the needle from the thread, tie a knot in the loose end, and clip the tail short. Tug gently from the spool end of the thread to bury the knot under the thread wrap. Complete your wraps, then cut the thread from the spool, leaving a few inches for finishing. Thread your needle and end off.

Starting with a cut length of thread is best when you will be taking stitches before ending off, rather than just wrapping the thread around the ball. First, cut the thread to a comfortable stitching length. This is usually 24" to 36," depending on the type of thread and your own preference. Thread the needle, tie a knot at the end, and cut the tail very short. Stick the point of the needle in the ball about 2" away from where you want the stitch to start. Slide the needle under the thread wrap and come up where you will start stitching. This is called *stitching underground*. Tug on the thread gently until the knot pops down under the thread wrap. If necessary, use the point of the needle to move the threads of the base wrap over the knot to cover it. Now you are ready to stitch the design.

Refine Your Skills To Knot or Not?

Experienced temari stitchers quickly develop a preference for knots or not, depending on the type of thread and purpose of the stitching. When placing guidelines on the ball or when using thin or slippery threads, start by anchoring the thread down into the ball with a knot. If you decide to eliminate the knot entirely, simply pull the cut end of the thread beneath the surface of the

ball. Alternatively, for a more secure start without a knot, make a few zigzag stitches back and forth under the ball's surface near the starting point. No matter what method you choose, make sure the thread is secure so that it does not easily pull out of the ball in the finished design.

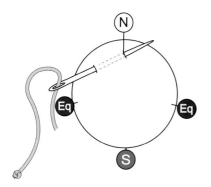
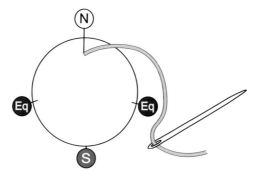

Start with cut thread: stitch underground to start point

Knot is hidden under thread wrap

Ending Off

No knot is required when ending your threads. Simply take a long underground stitch and clip the thread off at the surface of the ball. Make that last underground stitch deep into the ball so it will hold in place. If the thread is slippery or you want to make sure the ending-off stitch is extra secure, go back down in the same spot where the thread was brought up and make another underground stitch at an angle from the first one. Just before cutting the thread, apply a little tension and then snip. This will cause the underground stitch to retreat a little under the ball's surface. You can always use the point of your needle to groom the wrap threads to cover any end if needed.

Making Guidelines: Standard Temari Divisions

While it may seem that there are an infinite number of ways to place guidelines, temari making involves only four basic divisions that will allow for everything from simple to intricate designs. These are:

- Simple divisions, such as simple 4, simple 8, simple 10, simple 12, or simple 16 division (S4, S8, S10, S12, or S16), etc.

- Combination 8 division (C8)

- Combination 6 division (C6)

- Combination 10 division (C10)

In the text that follows, you will learn how to complete each of these divisions. Refer back to these pages to determine which division you will use for each temari you make.

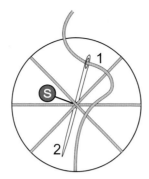 

Tack intersections

Tacking Intersections

When marking a ball, the intersections need to be tacked so that guidelines stay in place when you begin to stitch. For simple divisions, all of the intersections should be tacked in place. For combination divisions, all intersections with more than four threads should be tacked. Leave the guide pin in place until after the intersection is tacked.

There are two possibilities for tacking stitches: a starburst type of stitch and a simple diagonal stitch. Use your judgment and your eye to decide on a method—the goal is to make the intersection neat and secure regardless of the number of threads or the thickness of thread.

Starburst Tacking Stitch

Whether you are tacking just a few threads or many, the principle is the same. Take a small stitch across the intersection in between each of the marking threads. This means a four-way intersection is tacked with two stitches (a cross stitch); a six-way intersection requires three stitches, and so on. This method has the advantage of keeping all of the threads at the intersection evenly separated. The disadvantage is that it can be bulky with a larger thread. When you have selected a thick guideline thread or cord, consider tacking with a thinner thread that is the same color for a neater intersection.

Single Diagonal Tacking Stitch

This is the best method for tacking around the equator. Simply take one small diagonal stitch across the intersection. Make the stitch short but go deep enough into the thread wrap so that the stitch is securely anchored. For intersections with more threads, be sure you have an equal number of threads on each side of the tacking stitch. The advantage of this technique is that it is quick and neat. A disadvantage is that using a larger tacking thread can alter the spacing between the lines. In that case, carefully groom the threads to fix the spacing.

Tack As You Go

Tacking as you go saves time and thread. You can use either a small backstitch, similar to the single diagonal tacking stitch, or a series of stitches, similar to the starburst style of tacking. When adding vertical guidelines on the last wrap around the ball, pause when you reach the south pole and tack that intersection. Then keep wrapping on up to the north pole and tack there. This is not a good method for tacking the equator on simple divisions since it tends to make the equator line look staggered.

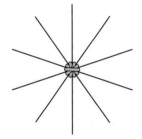

Starburst stitch

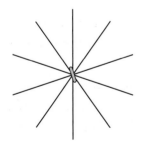

Diagonal stitch

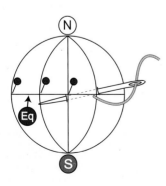

Tack equator

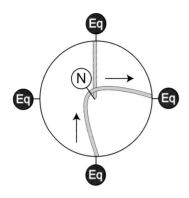

Step 2 Pivot at north pole

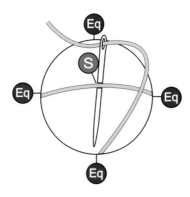

Step 3 Take backstitch at intersection

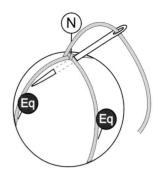

Step 4 Push needle toward equator

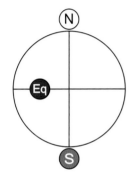

Completed S4 division

Simple Divisions

A simple division has a north pole and south pole with threads running vertically between them. It may or may not have an equator line wrapped around the middle. The division is named for the number of vertical guidelines it has; for instance, a simple 4 division (S4) has four vertical guidelines; S12 has twelve vertical guidelines, and so on. There are an infinite number of possible simple divisions limited only by the size of the ball and the size of your thread. Let's use an S4 division as an example of how to stitch guidelines for all simple divisions.

Simple 4 Division (S4)

1   Cut a paper strip to fit your ball and place pins for north pole, south pole, and four equator pins following the directions beginning on page 25.

2   Make the first guideline. Start your marking thread at the north pole (see Starting Your Thread on page 27). Wrap the thread around the ball, passing an equator pin as you go to the south pole, then passing another equator pin on the opposite side as you go back to the north pole. Pivot the thread around the north pole in order to make another wrap at the next equator pin.

3   Secure the pole intersections. Make your next wrap. As you pass the south pole, take a small backstitch to secure the intersection (see Tacking Intersections on page 30). Continue wrapping to the north pole and tack that intersection.

4   Stitch underground to an equator pin. Push the needle under the thread wrap at the north pole and slide it toward the equator. You may

S4 division   S6 division   S8 division

have to take several stitches underground to reach the equator pin. Come up next to a guideline and an equator pin.

5   Wrap and secure the equator. Wind the thread all the way around the ball at the equator, ending the thread at the same pin where you started. Tack all intersections and remove the equator pins. This is the perfect time to check that you did actually tack securely. The S4 division is now complete.

As you will find, simple divisions are the basis for many temari designs. They are also the first step in creating the more complex combination divisions that follow. Make sure you are expert in creating simple divisions before you proceed. Remember, practice, practice, practice!

Other Simple Divisions

The process for marking other simple divisions is the same as the S4 division, except with a different numbers of pins spaced evenly around the equator. When doubling the number of guidelines (S8, S16, etc.), use your paper measuring strip to determine where to place pins, folding the sections in half to get the required number of divisions. For S6, S10, or S12 divisions, it is easier to use a narrow centimeter tape measure than it is to fold the strip. First place the north pole, south pole, and equator pins and remove the paper strip from the ball. Measure the length of the strip in centimeters. Don't include the ¼" tab that you have at the north pole since that is not part of the total distance around. Divide by the number of vertical guidelines. Mark that measurement on your paper strip or pin the tape measure to the equator and use that to equally space the pins.

Make a Double C8

You can create a more intricately marked ball by adding more wrapped lines that begin at the equator. Cut a length of thread equal of four wraps around the ball, plus a few inches for starting and stopping. Come up at the intersection of the equator and one of the vertical guidelines that does not have C8 wraps. Add wraps straight around the ball, following the dashed lines in the diagram. Stitch underground to a similar equator intersection and complete.

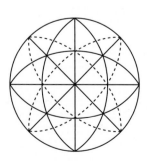

S10 division

S12 division

S16 division

Combination Divisions

Combination divisions are so named because they are essentially a combination of several simple divisions on the same ball. You can't create them with just any simple division. There are only three possible: the combination 8 (C8), the combination 6 (C6), and the combination 10 (C10). Each begins with a simple division; then extra guidelines are added which cross over the simple division guidelines and divide the ball into smaller shapes. These new shapes and intersections allow placement of designs all over the ball. Playing with the design possibilities of the different shapes is what keeps many temari stitchers intrigued for years!

C8 division

Combination 8 Division (C8)

A C8 division is easiest to mark if you keep track of the thread intersections by color coding the pins. Be sure to have plenty of simple division temari under your belt before tackling this one. You will be successful if you can already place the north and south pole pins directly opposite each other and accurately divide the equator into eight sections.

1   Begin with a ball marked in a S8 division (see Other Simple Divisions on page 32). Keep the white pin and blue pin marking the north and south poles in place. Insert black pins halfway between the poles and the equator on every other guideline.

2   Start your thread at the intersection of the equator and a guideline with black pins. Place a new black pin at this starting point. Wrap the thread all the way around the ball, using pins #1 and #2 as guides, back to the starting pin (red arrow indicates direction of thread).

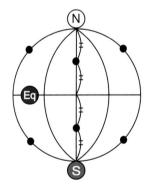

Step 1 Pin placement

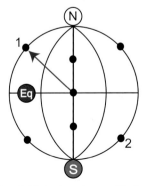

Step 2 Wrap thread around ball

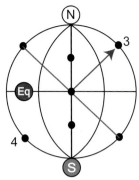

Step 3 Wrap in other direction

Step 4 Wrap thread around ball

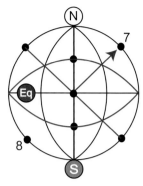

Step 5 Wrap in other direction

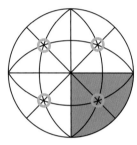

Step 6 Six-part triangle

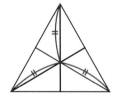

Long lines of six-part triangle

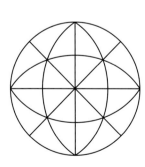

Complete

3 Pivot the thread around the pin at the starting point. Wrap the thread all the way around the ball, using pins #3 and #4 as guides (red arrow indicates direction of thread). Tack the intersection at the starting point. Remove the starting point pin and pins #1 through #4.

4 Stitch underground to come up at the intersection of the equator and another guideline between two black pins. Place a black pin at this starting point. Wrap around the ball using pins #5 and #6 as guides.

5 Pivot the thread around the starting pin and wrap around the ball using pins #7 and #8 as guides.

6 Tack all intersections at the equator. If needed, adjust the guidelines by sliding them a bit to create equally sized shapes on the ball. Pay particular attention to the shaded triangle on the diagram. It is made up of six smaller triangles and is called a *six-part triangle*. Lines from the center of the six-part triangle to the points are longer than the lines from the center to the sides. Check that the long lines within the six-part triangle are the same length by measuring or judging the distance by eye. Tack the six-way intersections at the triangle centers (orange circles in the drawing). Your C8 division is now complete and you are ready to stitch the design.

Combination 6 Division (C6)

The C6 division is essentially a C8 division with some of the guidelines removed. It can be made by starting with a simple 6 division but the method described here is much easier and has the same result. The C6 is particularly useful when you want to create a design with four

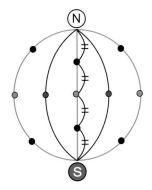
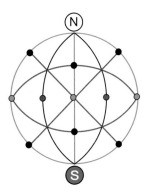
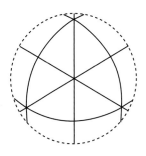

Step 2 Pin placement   Step 3 Wrap diagonal lines   Step 4 Complete

equally spaced design centers. You should be very familiar with marking a
C8 division before attempting a C6. To mark a C6 division, you'll mark a C8
division using regular guideline thread for some of the lines and scrap thread
(which will be removed) for the others.

1   First wrap four of the vertical guidelines as in an S4 division (see page
31) and end off. Wrap the four remaining vertical guidelines in scrap
thread. Use green pins to mark the equator on the four vertical guidelines
wrapped with scrap thread. Use red pins for the other guidelines. Do not
wrap a line for the equator.

2   Place black pins halfway between poles and equator on the vertical
guidelines wrapped with scrap thread (green lines on diagram).

3   Wrap the diagonal lines from the equator as if you were marking a C8.
Use regular marking thread, not scrap thread. Begin at the equator next to a
green pin on a line of scrap thread and wrap two complete times around the
ball. Stitch underground to the other green pin at the equator and wrap the
remaining two diagonal wraps (red lines on diagram).

4   Adjust the lines just as you would for a C8 division, then remove the scrap
thread. Tack all intersections. You will have 8 six-way intersections and 6 four-
way intersections. Rotate the ball so you can find the large triangle. This is
the usual orientation for C6 diagrams. Since the C6 division does not have an
equator line, it is shown here with a dashed line for the outer circle.

Four Tops, photographed on page 166, is a design built on C6 division
guidelines.

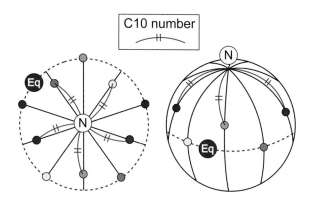

Step 2 Move half of pins to north

Tips for Wrapping the Guidelines

Wrap snugly so the guideline thread remains taut when you are stitching the design but not so snugly that it indents the surface of the ball. As you wrap, lay guideline thread in a straight line, from pin to pin. When you need to pivot around a pin or take a stitch with the needle, hold the guideline thread in place with the thumb of your non-stitching hand to keep the thread taut.

Make sure each vertical guideline thread is on the same side of the equator pin. The small distance of a pin width might make a difference in the final accuracy of your marking in more intricate designs. This is easy to do by laying the thread to the right side of the equator pin that you pass as you wrap from north towards the south, and to the left side of the equator pin that you pass as you wrap from south to north.

Combination 10 Division (C10)

Learn to mark a C10 division and you will discover a whole new realm of exciting and fascinating temari patterns. This division has twelve pentagons nested side by side, perfect for filling with stars or flowers. There are several methods that can be used for marking a C10. If you are new to this process, start with the S10 version on the next page. In all methods you will need to measure and place pins to mark the centers of the twelve pentagons. This requires finding a special distance known as the magic number or the C10 number. It truly seems magical that using this one distance helps you create such beautiful symmetry with your guidelines.

Finding the Magic C10 Number In order to mark a C10 division you need to figure the distance between the pentagon centers on your ball. This is the C10 number and it is used to adjust the location of the pins to mark the twelve pentagon centers on the ball. You can calculate it directly using a simple formula or you can look up the value in the chart on page 180.

First, measure the circumference of your ball. If you are using the chart, use either the table on the right side of the number chart or use the scale on the left side to find the C10 number. For example, if the circumference is 30 cm, the C10 number is 5.3 cm.

If you don't have the chart handy, or you need the C10 number for a circumference that is not on the chart, you will need to calculate the number directly. Use this formula:

C10 number = (circumference ÷ 6) + (circumference ÷ 100)

For a 30 cm ball you would get:

C10 number = (30 ÷ 6) + (30 ÷ 100) = 5 + .3 = 5.3 cm.

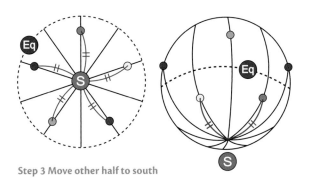
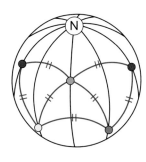

Step 3 Move other half to south   Step 4 Measure and adjust   Step 5 Add wraps at green pins

Marking an C10 Division from a S10 division

1   Mark an S10 division by placing the north and south pole pins in the ball as usual. Add ten pins equally spaced around the equator using pins in five different colors (green, yellow, red, purple, and blue). Place the same colors opposite each other on the ball. Wrap the vertical guidelines, dividing the ball into a S10 division and end off. *Do not* wrap a guideline around the equator. There are now twelve pins in the ball. Next, you will move the equator pins so that all twelve pins are the same distance apart.

2   Find your C10 number. Measure this distance down from the north pole and reposition half of the equator pins, one of each color, towards the north pole.

3   Measuring from the south pole, use the same C10 number to move the remaining pins towards the south pole.

4   Spend some time measuring between the twelve pins on the ball, checking to make sure they are equally spaced. Reposition them as necessary. They may be off a bit if the ten vertical guidelines are not quite straight. Sometimes, you can move a pin to the other side of a guideline or adjust the C10 number up or down slightly. Try to get the pins to within 2 mm of the C10 number.

5   Measure a length of guideline thread equal to four wraps around the ball, plus about 8" for starting and stopping. Knot one end and then bring the thread up at a green pin. Find the green pin on the other side of the ball (directly opposite). Wrap one time straight around the ball laying the thread next to a blue pin, the green pin directly opposite, the other blue pin, and back to the starting point. Pivot around the starting

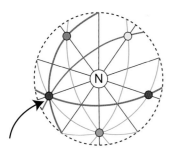

Step 6 Add wraps at red pins

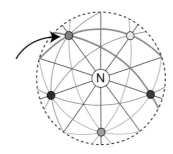

Step 7 Add wraps at blue pins

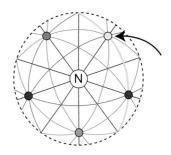

Step 8 Add wrap at remaining pins

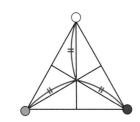

Step 9 Six-part triangle

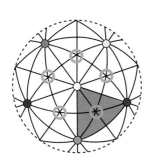

Tack triangle centers

point and continue to wrap and add new guidelines until you have ten guideline threads intersecting at each of the green pins. With each new wrap, you lay the thread next to one of the other colored pins and the green pin on the opposite side of the ball. End off.

6   Using the same starting and stopping techniques as in Step 5, begin at a red pin and add wraps until you have ten guideline threads intersecting at each of the red pins. This time you will add three full wraps around the ball since the lines for the green pins are already there.

7   Using the same starting and stopping techniques as in Step 5, begin at a blue pin and add wraps until you have ten guideline threads intersecting at each of the blue pins. This time you will add two full wraps around the ball since the lines for the green and red pins are already there.

8   Add one last guideline wrapped next to the pair of yellow pins so that you have ten guideline threads intersecting at each of the yellow and purple pins. Now, each of the twelve centers on the ball has an intersection of ten threads.

9   Tack the threads crossing through the intersections at the pentagon centers. These are the spots where your colored pins are located. Next, adjust the guidelines by sliding them as needed to create equal-sized shapes on the ball. Pay particular attention to each six–part triangle. Check that the long lines within the triangle are the same length by measuring or judging the distance by eye. Tack the triangle centers (orange circles in the drawing). Your C10 division is now complete and you are ready to stitch the design.

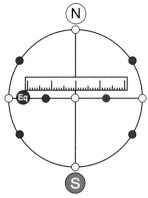

Step 2 Place red pins on each side of white pin

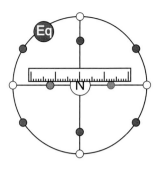

Step 3 Place blue pins at north and south

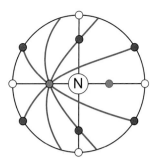

Step 4 Wrap to create ten way intersections

Marking a C10 Division from an S4 Division

This method of marking a C10 is for more advanced temari stitchers who are already adept at marking a C10 beginning with an S10 division and are familiar with the shapes on a C10. This method is fast and accurate.

1   Mark an S4 division with an equator line (see page 31) using all white pins. Do not tack the intersections. Make sure the guidelines run straight from pin to pin. A C10 division temari has twelve centers that are equally spaced. The white pins already in the ball are *not* at the twelve pentagon centers. They will be at the centers of the diamonds when the division is complete. You will add colored pins for the pentagon centers in the next steps.

2   To figure out where to put the first pair of colored pins, divide the C10 number in half. Use that distance to place a red pin on each side of one of the white pins on the equator. When you measure from red pin to red pin, that distance should be the C10 number. Rotate the ball one guideline to the right and place one red pin above and below the equator intersection. Continue to place pairs of red pins, alternating horizontally and vertically for the other two intersections on the equator.

3   Place pairs of blue pins by the north pole and by the south pole. These pins will be on the vertical guidelines that do not have red pins. When all twelve colored pins are in place, spend some time checking that they are all equally spaced (using the C10 number). It is likely that you will need to adjust them a bit.

4   Wrap guidelines next to a blue pin. The twelve colored pins will be the pentagon centers of the C10 marking so you need to create a ten-way intersection of threads at each of these colored pins. Start at

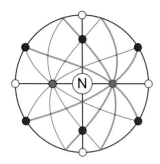

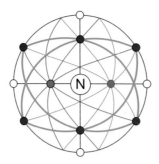

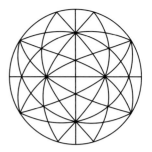

Step 5 Wrap guidelines at other blue pin

Step 6 Continue adding wraps at red pins

Step 7 Complete: four-part diamond is in center and facing forward

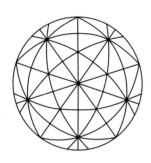

Step 7 Complete: ten-part pentagon is facing forward

one of the blue pins next to the north pole. Find the blue pin directly opposite (near the south pole) to see where you are headed when you wrap. Wrap straight around the ball, past a red pin, past a blue pin near the south pole, past a red pin, and back to where you started. Ignore the white pins. Pivot and continue wrapping until you have created ten-way intersections at your starting pin and the blue pin directly opposite (next to the south pole). End off.

5 Wrap guidelines at the other blue pin. Start at the blue pin on the other side of the north pole. Wrap and pivot until you have created ten-way intersections at your starting pin and the blue pin directly opposite (next to the south pole). End off.

6 Wrap guidelines for the red pins located around the equator area. These pins will already have some of their lines; you will just need to add the ones needed to complete the ten-way intersections. Bring your thread up at a red pin and wrap straight around the ball next to the appropriate red pins. Continue adding wraps until each colored pin on the ball has a ten-way intersection of guidelines. End off.

7 Tack the intersections at each of the colored pins on the ball. Then adjust the shapes and tack the triangle centers (see Step 9 on page 38). You can now remove the white pins, being careful to tack if necessary.

Have you learned to tack as you go (page 30)? Use your time efficiently and save thread. During the process of wrapping guidelines on the C10 with any of these methods, each time you apply the last wrap that completes a ten-way intersection of threads, take a moment to tack that intersection. Then continue wrapping, tacking each completed intersection as you go.

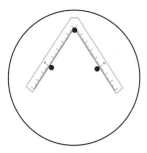

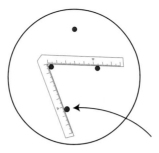

Step 1 Use v-ruler to place three pins   **Step 2 Reposition to place fourth pin**

Marking a C10 Division Using a V-Ruler

There is one more method for marking a C10 division. In this technique, you use a v-ruler to space twelve pins equally around the ball before applying any guidelines. V-rulers can be obtained from sources that specialize in temari making supplies. (See page 178.)

1   Measure your ball and figure the C10 number. Place a pin anywhere in the ball and position the center of the v-ruler around it. This pin is the first of your twelve C10 centers. Lay the legs of the ruler down along the curve of the ball, keeping it hooked on that first pin and trying not to distort the 72 degree angle of the ruler. Hold only the legs and don't force down the bottom part of the "V" on the other side of the pin. That part of the ruler will stick up a little. Measure along an inside leg of the v-ruler and place a pin there. Then measure along the other inside leg of the v-ruler and place a pin there. You now have three pins in the ball, equally spaced. The distance between each of them is the C10 number.

2   Reposition the ruler so it is around two of the three pins. One pin is at the center of the "V" and the other pin is on an inside leg. Check to make sure the distance between these is the C10 number. Measure out along the other inside leg of the ruler and place a fourth pin there.

3   Continue to reposition the ruler, measure, and place pins until you have all twelve pins in the ball. Wrap guidelines around the ball so that each pin has a ten-way intersection of threads. Tack as usual.

Using Temari Diagrams

A key part of understanding temari patterns is being able to read a temari diagram. This is a useful skill not only for English language patterns but also for patterns that you may find in other sources, such as the many available Japanese books. Learning to read a temari diagram will help you to decipher designs that you see in pictures when there are no text instructions to guide you. By comparing the pictured design to standard diagram layouts, you can often determine what division was used to mark the ball, whether or not support lines were added, and which shapes were used to stitch the elements of the design.

Understanding temari diagrams can also help you to plan your own designs by allowing you to try out ideas and look at shapes in a different context. Copy blank versions of the diagrams from the appendix (pages 181 and 182) and use colored pencils to try out your design ideas before committing to needle and thread.

The standards used for the diagrams in this book are common to many other temari sources. In general, solid black lines represent the actual guidelines on the ball. Dashed lines can represent either imaginary reference lines (such as an equator that does not have a guideline) or support lines that are added after the initial division (see the next section). Colored or thicker lines are used to show the actual stitched parts of the design.

Look for fraction lines to show placement of design motifs. These will look like bumps next to a marking line with small hash marks to show equivalent sections. Thus, all lines with one hash mark are equal to each other and all lines with two hash marks are equal to each other, and so on.

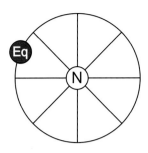

North pole view

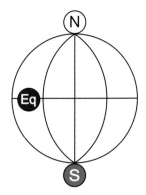

Side view

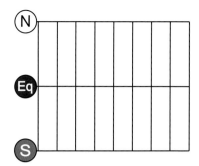

Rectangular diagram

Simple Division Diagrams

Simple divisions can be represented with round or rectangular diagrams. A rectangular diagram represents the vertical guidelines as vertical lines. The north and south poles are shown as lines across the top and bottom. The three diagrams above are for an S8 division with equator. Notice the round diagram can be shown with either a north pole view or a side view.

C6 Division Diagrams

The dominant shape on a C6 is a large six-part triangle. Like the C8, there are also squares and diamonds, but they are not commonly used in C6 designs. The usual view for a C6 diagram is with the triangle centered. Note that the outermost circle of the diagram is a dashed line because there is no guideline there on the actual division.

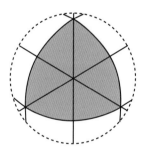

C6 with large six-part triangles

Refine Your Skills Exploring Different Markings

You can improve your understanding of different divisions by stitching similar designs on marked balls. For example, look for the six-part triangles and fill them with tri-wings (stitch individually or as continuous paths). You will find these triangles on all the combination divisions. Then, stitch open shapes. On the C6, stitch open triangles in each remaining six-part triangle. On the C8, stitch open squares in each eight-part square. On the C10, stitch open pentagons in each ten-part pentagon.

Triangles on C6

Squares on C8

Pentagons on C10

Combination Division Diagrams

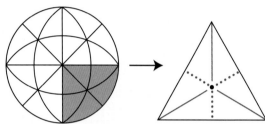

With 6 eight-part squares on the ball

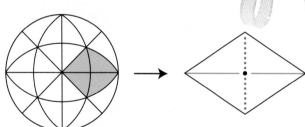

With 8 six-part triangles on the ball

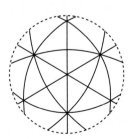

With 12 four-part diamonds on the ball

View with triangle at center

C8 Division Diagrams

Temari pattern directions for designs stitched on a C8 division often refer you to the square, triangle, or diamond shapes formed by the guidelines.

Locate the lines within each shape and notice that there are two different lengths. The short lines go from the center of the shape to the side of the shape (dotted lines in these diagrams). The long lines go from the center of the shape to the corner of the shape. Learn to recognize these shapes and lines for exact placement of design stitches.

C10 Division Diagrams

The most obvious shape on a C10 division is the pentagon that surrounds each of the twelve centers. Just as on the C8, there are triangles and diamonds with each shape having short and long lines. The short lines go from the center of the shape to the side of the shape (dotted lines in these diagrams). The long lines go from the center of the shape to the corner of the shape. Learn to recognize these shapes and the lines for exact placement of design stitches.

C10 diagrams are commonly presented as a round view with a pentagon in the center. An alternative view of a C10 division is flattened so that the lines are drawn as straight segments. This is a useful view when it is necessary to show both sides of the ball or when the design is mostly centered on the pentagons.

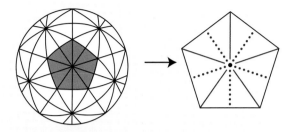

With 12 ten-part pentagons

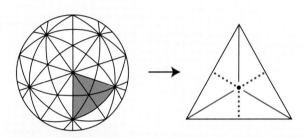

With 20 six-part triangles

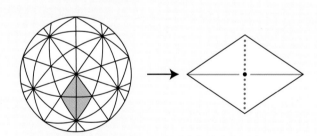

With 30 four-part diamonds

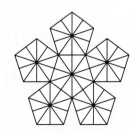

Flat view of C10

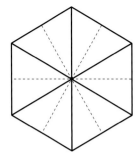

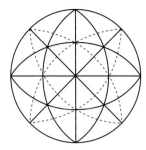

Subdivide a single shape   Look for a continuous path

Adding Support Guidelines

Temari designs with extra guidelines often seem very intricate and, at first glance, intimidating to the stitcher. Yet with just a few extra steps, you can transform a single shape on the ball or an entire division into a more complex grid that is ready for stitching smaller designs. With your choice of thread, you decide whether the support lines become the main focus of the design or fade into the background where their purpose is to help you place design stitches. Either way, design possibilities will bloom as you explore the many options for adding extra guidelines.

Before adding support lines to any division, either simple or combination, make sure you already have a lot of experience with that division. It often helps to create a larger ball and use finer thread for the guidelines so you have plenty of room for your design. Support lines are dashed lines in the diagrams while the regular division lines are solid.

Subdividing a Single Shape

Want to stitch a flower with twelve petals in a hexagon? Simply use the same guideline thread and stitch from side to side so you have a twelve-way intersection in the center. Stitch underground, beneath the shape, to begin each new line. Tack the center as the final step. Use the same technique to add shapes within a shape.

Subdividing Multiple Shapes with a Continuous Path

When subdividing several adjacent shapes or even the entire temari, look for a continuous path (see page 129) that can be stitched or wrapped through several of the shapes. When wrapping, you may need to stitch into the ball or tack new intersections to keep support lines in place.

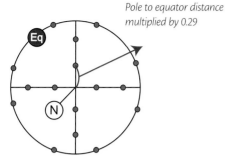

Pole to equator distance multiplied by 0.29

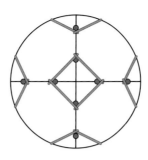

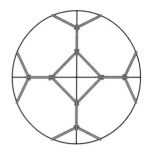

Step 2 Multiply by 0.29   Step 3 Stitch one row   Connect all shapes

Subdividing Simple Division Temari

A simple division can become a unique puzzle with squares, hexagons, pentagons, and diamonds nested side by side. Each of these shapes is called a *face*. Add support lines to outline the shapes and then add more to subdivide each shape to suit your design ideas. There are so many options!

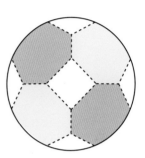

Step 4 Complete

14 Faces Method #1 Transform an S4 division into a temari with six squares and eight hexagons. Use this method when you plan to fill the shapes with free embroidery, swirls, weaving, or other designs that do not need guidelines.

1 Mark the ball in an S4 division using scrap thread (sewing thread or other thin thread used to temporarily mark the ball).

2 Measure the distance from a pole to the equator. Multiply by 0.29. Place pins this distance out from the pole on each of the four division lines. Repeat around each intersection on the ball.

3 With your selected guideline thread, stitch one row around each square. With the same guideline thread, stitch long, straight stitches between the corners of the squares so all shapes are connected. Remove the pins as you go.

5 Remove the scrap thread and your marking is complete.

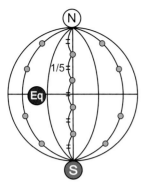

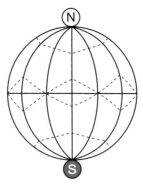

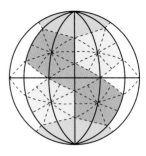

Step 2 Place pins on alternate vertical guidelines

Step 3 Diamond pattern

Step 4 Add support lines

20 Faces Method #1 Transform an S12 division into a temari with two hexagons (one at each pole), twelve pentagons (six around each hexagon), and six diamonds (at the equator).

1 Mark an S12 with an equator with your selected guideline thread.

2 Measure from the north pole to south pole and divide by five. Place pins on every other vertical guideline at 1/5, 2/5, 3/5 and 4/5.

3 With your selected guideline thread, stitch a hexagon around the six pins surrounding each pole. Then stitch zigzag paths over the equator to create diamonds as shown in the diagram. Tack the threads at the points of the diamonds where they cross at the equator.

4 Add support lines as desired within each shape to stitch your design.

Desert Spirit, photographed here and with an alternate view on page 16, is an example of a temari marked with 20 faces. The diamonds around the equator are filled with dense pine needle stitching (page 63). The hexagons and pentagons contain various herringbone designs (pages 95 to 107). It is amazing how many unique designs you can fit on a ball like this. It is a great way to experiment with different patterns—and it makes an exquisite gift or ornament when you have finished.

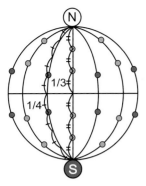

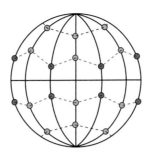

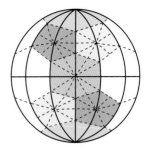

Step 2 Place pins   Step 3 Stitch zigzag pattern   Step 4 Add support lines

20 Faces Method #2   Transform an S12 into a ball with two
hexagons (at poles), twelve pentagons (six around each hexagon), and six
more hexagons (on equator).

1   Mark an S12 with an equator using your selected guideline thread.

2   Measure from the pole to the equator and divide by three. Place
green pins on every other vertical guideline at 1/3 and 2/3 above and
below the equator. Then measure from the pole to the equator and divide
by 4. Place blue pins at quarter distance above and below the equator pin
on the vertical guidelines not used before.

3   With your selected guideline thread, stitch a hexagon around the six
pins surrounding each pole. Stitch a zigzag path (red dashed line in the
diagram) connecting the blue pins with the remaining green pins above
the equator. Then stitch a similar zigzag path below the equator.

4   Add support lines as desired within each shape to stitch your design.

Subdividing C8 Division Temari

Just as with the simple divisions, you can add support lines to a C8 and
end up with some surprising results. Pentagons on a C8? Yes, it can be
done, and this marking is as intriguing as design stitching. Again, many
possibilities exist and the ones that follow are some favorite puzzles.

14 Faces Method #2   This method begins with a C8 division
temari. The six squares and eight hexagons that you create have
guidelines which meet in the centers of the shapes. Use this for stitches
like a kiku herringbone where you'll work around the center.

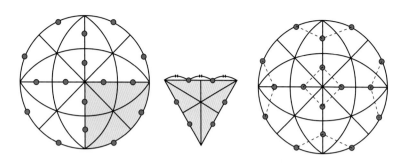
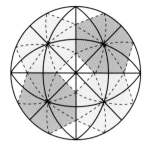

Step 2 Place pins   Step 3 Stitch square around pins   Step 4 Add more support lines

1 Mark the ball in a C8 division using your selected guideline thread.

2 Place two guide pins along the sides of each six-part triangle to divide each side into three equal sections.

3 With your guideline thread, stitch a square around the four pins in each eight-part square.

4 Find the hexagons in between the squares and add more support lines as desired for stitching a more intricate design.

16 Faces Transform a C8 division into a temari with four regular hexagons and twelve slightly elongated pentagons.

1 Mark a C8 division using your selected guideline thread. Place pins #1 and #2 in the centers of the six-part triangles diagonally opposite the north pole. Then place pins #3 and #4 in the centers of the six-part triangles diagonally opposite at the south pole. Each of these four pins will be at the center of a triangle, creating a four centers marking. They are equidistant. Next, measure the length of a short line of a six-part triangle surrounding one of the four pins. Place red pins out from the triangle center that same distance along the long lines. Also place red pins at the ends of the short lines, along the triangle's edge. You should now have six red pins which form a hexagon.

2 Stitch support lines around the red pins to form a hexagon around each of the four centers. Remove the pins as you go.

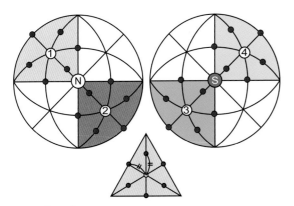

Step 1 Place pins

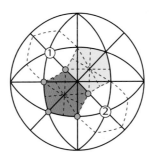

Steps 2 and 3 Form hexagons
and locate pentagons

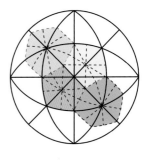

Step 4 Add support lines to
divide into ten parts

3 Next, look for pentagons between the hexagons you have just outlined. In the drawing, there is a blue pentagon with green pins at its points. There is a yellow pentagon next to it. There will be two guidelines already running through each pentagon that you may disregard. The pentagons are not quite regular in shape (they do not have equal sides and angles). You can nudge the intersections a bit in order to visually even the shapes. Add support lines to divide each pentagon into ten parts.

4 Follow the same process on the other side of the ball around pins #3 and #4. Then, looking at the shapes that remain, you will find eight pentagons arranged around the equator. Add support lines to all pentagons to divide into ten parts.

18 Faces Transform a C8 division into a temari with six squares and twelve slightly elongated hexagons.

1 Mark the ball in a C8 division using your selected guideline thread.

2 Divide each side of the four-part diamonds in half and mark with a pin.

3 Stitch around the pins to make a small square within each eight–part square.

4 Find the hexagons in between the squares and add support lines to subdivide each of these shapes.

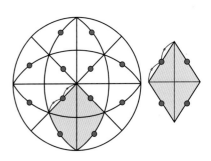

Step 2 Place pins

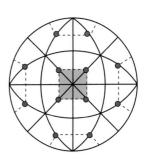

Step 3 Stitch square around pins

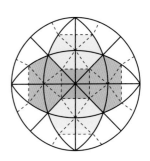

Step 4 Add support lines

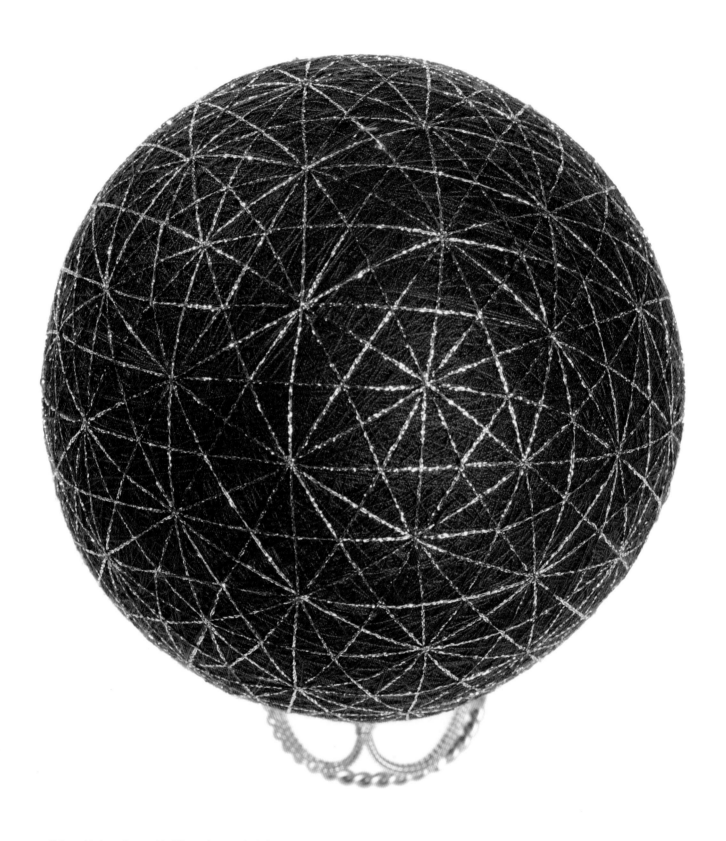

This sophisticated temari ball is made up entirely from guidelines.
Support lines are added to a C10 division, using the diamond-
based method described on page 55.

Marking 32 centers: Place pins for
32 centers as shown in the diagram.
Stitch a five-point star inside each of
the C10 pentagons. Place stitches on
the pentagon's long lines. Tack.

Marking 42 centers: Place pins
for 42 centers as shown in the
diagram. Stitch a five-point star
inside each of the C10 pentagons.
Place stitches on the pentagon's
short lines. Tack.

Marking Multi-Centers (Subdividing C10)

Multi-centers, the ultimate marking, create a multitude of tiny
hexagons on the temari. You will always have twelve pentagons, as
on the original C10. However, as you divide the ball further, those
pentagons will become smaller to make room for more hexagons.
Use an attractive thread for your guidelines and the marking itself
can become the only design on the ball. Or, mark the ball, then fill
each pentagon and hexagon with the same motif and you'll have
a repetitive design displaying an attractive symmetry. Advanced
stitchers enjoy looking for unique combinations and arrangements of
shapes suitable for intricate geometric or floral designs.

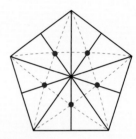

32 centers

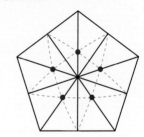

42 centers

You can use one of two different methods for measuring where
to place the support lines for multi-centers on a C10 division temari,
based either on the triangle or the diamond. The different methods
create slightly different orientations of the shapes on the ball. The
process is as simple as measuring the side of the shape and placing
pins to divide the sides into sections. The more sections you mark
along each side, the more hexagons you'll create. Then stitch around
these pins with your guideline thread to subdivide the each shape.
You're done!

This is a quick overview of how to mark some basic multi-
centers. After the pins are in place, there are many possible stitching
paths to add the support lines. Here you'll find a stitching path for
each method, triangle or diamond-based, that always works. After
you learn these paths and become familiar with the multi-center
concept and technique, explore other paths which might save time
or thread. They will certainly provide hours of "puzzling" fun.

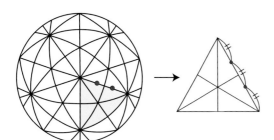

Step 2 Place pins

Triangles

Step 3 Stitch two pentagons

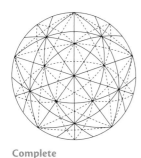

Complete

Triangle Based Multis

1   Decide how many centers you want to create and use this chart for pin placement. Repeat for all triangles on the ball.

Divide each side by	# centers total
3	32
6	122
9	272
12	482

2   Find a six-part triangle on the ball. Measure the length of one side of the triangle. Place pins to divide the side into sections. This first example shows dividing the triangle side into three sections for a 32 centers marking. Repeat for all triangles on the ball.

3   After all the pins are in place, stitch two pentagons around one of the C10 centers, connecting the pins and removing them as you go.

4   Repeat, stitching pentagons around each of the twelve centers on the C10. Tack where necessary. This completes your 32 centers marking.

For other triangle-based markings, follow the same process. First divide the triangle side into sections. For example, for 122 centers, divide each triangle side into six sections. Place pins, then stitch pentagons around the pins. Next, stitch pentagons around each of the twelve centers on the C10, tacking where necessary. This completes a 122 centers marking.

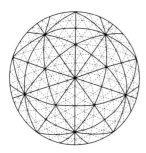

122 centers

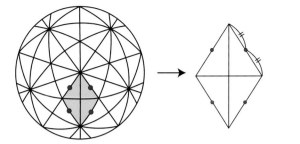

Step 2 Place pins

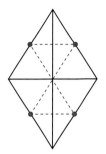

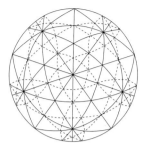

Step 3 Stitch in one diamond

42 centers

Diamond Based Multis

1 Decide how many centers to create and use this chart for pin placement.

Divide each line by	# centers total
2	42
3	92
4	162
5	252

2 Find a four-part diamond on the ball. Measure the length of one side of the diamond. Place pins to divide all four sides of the diamond into sections. This first example shows dividing each diamond side into two sections for a 42 centers marking.

3 Working in just one diamond, stitch between the pins to create small triangles as shown in the diagram. Repeat Steps 2 and 3 for each diamond on the ball. Your 42 centers marking is complete.

For other diamond-based markings, follow the same process. First divide the diamond side into sections. For example, for 92 centers, divide each diamond side into three sections. Place pins, then stitch between the pins in one diamond. Next, fill in the remaining diamonds.

While the stitching on multi-centers temari often seems intricate and complex, you can usually break the process down into repetitions of the same motif stitched in the hexagons and pentagons. You could stitch open basic shapes, which are interlocked or layered over the entire ball. Or you could fill each hexagon and pentagon with a solid shape or a small herringbone motif. Try to stretch your design skills by sectioning off parts of the ball—such as groups of pentagons, hexagons, triangles, or diamonds—and fill each of these as one unit.

Multi-Center Design Idea

Here's another design idea. Section off the bottom part of the ball and fill it with basketweave. Use the shapes just above the rim of the basket as guides to stitch flowers, using free embroidery or solid shapes. Fill the area around the top of the ball with kites shapes and clouds by stitching solid basic shapes.

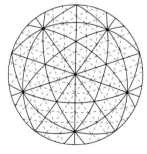

92 centers

Simple Stitching and Wrapping Techniques

Let your exploration of temari embroidery techniques begin

with stitches that you may already know from other types of

embroidery. All the basics are covered here, along with ideas

for you to try out to improve your stitching. You'll learn how

to hold the ball in one hand while stitching with the other, and

how to start and end off your thread—simple skills that take

a just a bit of practice. In this chapter, stitching and wrapping

techniques are sequenced from easy to more challenging.

The patterns, too, start simple and progress to more intricate

combinations of stitches and techniques.

Surface Embroidery Stitches *(Shishū)*

While traditional temari designs often include stitches unique to the craft, you can decorate your thread-wrapped ball with many familiar surface embroidery stitches or, in Japanese, *shishū*.

The main difference between working on a temari and embroidering on fabric is that with temari, you have no access to the wrong side of the work. For that reason, sewn stitches like stem stitch and chain stitch are easier than stabbed stitches like French knots. With a little ingenuity however, almost all surface embroidery stitches can be used on temari to create beautiful designs. Take care to plan your exit point from the ball each time you begin a stitch. Aim for exiting at the spot where you would like your next stitch to begin. If this is

Opposite: Like candy in a jar!

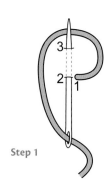

Step 1

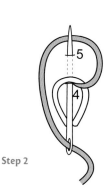

Step 2

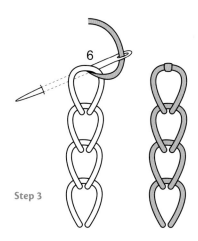

Step 3

too awkward, just stitch under the thread-wrapped layer an inch or so away in any direction and come up. Then reenter the ball in the same spot and stitch back to the design area to add more embroidery. As you stitch, remember to handle the ball gently to avoid loosening the thread-wrapped layer. Review the tips for starting with a cut length of thread on page 28.

Chain Stitch

1 Begin with an underground stitch, coming up at 1. Lay the thread in a loop to form a chain link (hold in place with your thumb). Insert the needle at 2 (very close to 1) and exit a short distance away at 3.

2 Gently pull the stitch through. Insert the needle at 4 (very close to the exit point of the previous stitch) and come up a short distance away at 5.

3 Continue adding links as desired. End off by going down at 6 and coming up a few inches away. Clip the thread tail at the surface of the ball.

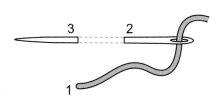

Step 1 Begin cross stitch

Cross Stitch

1 Begin with an underground stitch and come up at 1. Stitch from 2 to 3.

2 Complete the cross stitch by entering the ball at 4 and exiting a couple of inches away at 5. Clip the thread close to the surface of the ball.

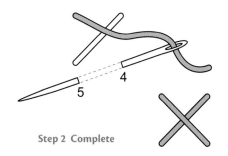

Step 2 Complete

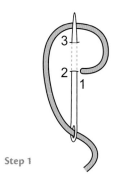

Step 1

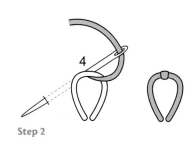

Step 2

Detached Chain or Lazy Daisy

1   Begin with an underground stitch, coming up at 1. Lay the thread in a loop to form a chain link (hold in place with your thumb). Insert the needle at 2 (very close to 1) and exit a short distance away at 3.

2   Gently pull the stitch through. Insert the needle at 4, just outside last link, and come up about 2" away in any direction. Pull the stitch through the ball and clip the thread tail at the surface of the ball.

Stem Stitch

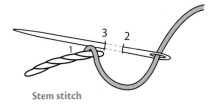

Stem stitch

1   Working from left to right, make small, straight stitches in a line. Come up at 1, hold the working thread below the needle, and then stitch from 2 to 3.

2   End off by stitching away a couple of inches in any direction. Clip the thread close to the surface of the ball.

Couching

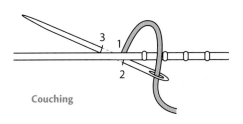

Couching

Use this technique to attach thick decorative thread, cord, or ribbon to the temari. Lay the decorative thread along your desired path and tack in place with a thinner thread. Come up at 1 and stitch around and under the decorative thread by going down at 2 and coming up at 3.

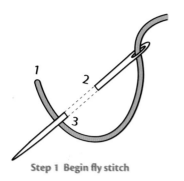

Step 1 Begin fly stitch

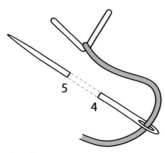

Step 2

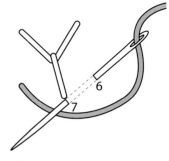

Step 3

Fly Stitch

1 Begin with an underground stitch and come up at 1. Stitch from 2 to 3 to form the first "V".

2 Stitch from 4 to 5 to make the first part of the stem.

3 Stitch from 6 to 7 to make the next "V".

4 Repeat this sequence until the stem is the desired length. Then end off by going down at 8 and coming up a couple of inches away in any direction. Clip the thread close to the surface of the ball.

French Knot

1 Begin with an underground stitch and come up at 1. Wind the thread 2 or 3 times around the needle.

2 Insert needle back into temari at 2 (very close to the spot where you began). Exit at 3, a couple of inches away in any direction.

3 Slowly pull the thread through, holding the knot gently with your thumb to keep it in place. Clip the thread close to the surface of the ball.

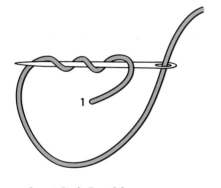

Step 1 Begin French knot

Step 2

Complete

MUMS PATTERN

26 cm (10 ¼") ball wrapped with off-white

Sample photographed (front): Maxi-Lock Eggshell (off-white); DMC # 5 perle cotton: 3348 (light green), 224 (light pink), 225 (very light pink), and 223 (pink)

Combine some of these embroidery stitches to place sprays of mums randomly around the temari. Choose shades of light green, light pink, and very light pink perle cotton.

1 Begin with light green. Make the stem and branches with a single straight stitch and then fly stitches.

2 To create each flower, begin with light pink and stitch a group of six lazy daisy stitches around a center.

3 Change thread to very light pink and stitch lazy daisy stitches between each of the original ones. Vary the size and angle placement of these looped stitches for an interesting effect. In the center of each flower, stitch a French knot (with two wraps around the needle) with pink.

4 Complete three or four flowers for each stem.

Step 1

Step 2   Step 3

Step 4

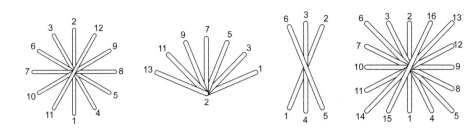

Pineneedle variation

Pine Needle Stitching (Matsuba Kagari)

Pine needle stitching can be used as the main part of your design or it can be used to embellish any unstitched areas, called *negative space*. At their simplest, pine needle stitches are a series of long straight stitches that cross in the center. They vary in structure from full circles to partial circles and fans. Change the shape by changing the length of the individual stitches to match the shape you want to fill. Tacking the center of a pine needle design is an option. Each of the diagrams here shows a different possibility. Bring your needle up at odd numbers and go down into the ball at even numbers.

Dense Pine Needles

Making a pine needle design with a lot of stitches or with thick thread can create too much bulk in the center. To overcome this, stitch part of the design as usual with all stitches equally spaced. Tack the center. When you add stitches between each of the original ones, stitch under the tacking stitch in the center and down into the thread wrap to reduce the bulk. Use a sharp needle and a thimble.

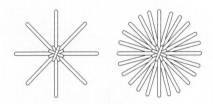

PINE SHAPES PATTERN

Any size ball wrapped with off white

Sample photographed opposite: Maxi-Lock Eggshell; Rainbow Gallery Treasure Braid Petite PB201 (metallic yellow); Kyo perle rayon: 524 (light purple), 16 (medium purple), and 17 (dark purple). (Note: Kyo thread is available by special order from Japan)

1   Begin by marking a C8 division with metallic yellow (see page 33).

2   Select shapes made by the guidelines and fill with pine needle stitching, either squares, triangles, or diamonds. Tack the centers.

3   Outline the shapes with a row of metallic yellow.

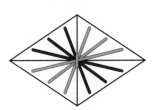
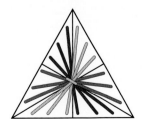

Opposite: Pine needle variations

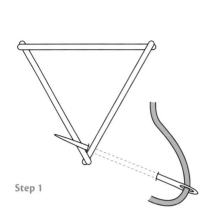

Step 1

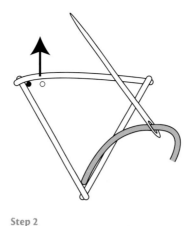

Step 2

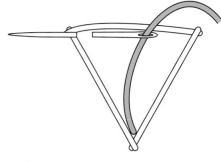

Step 3

Swirl Stitching (Uzumaki Kagari)

Any shape on the temari can be filled with swirl stitching. The technique is very easy and no guidelines are required. Swirls is a densely stitched design, so make certain that the thread wrap on your temari is tight and thick so your stitches stay in place and do not collapse toward the center of the shape. Your goal is to be consistent: make each stitch the same length, stitch with your needle set parallel to the previous row, and exit as close as you can to the corner of the previous row. When all of the swirl stitching is complete, you may see a gap where you wish the threads were closer together. You can fill in the gap by adding a single, carefully placed stitch.

1   Stitch the outline of the desired shape, making the stitches as short as you can for sharp points. To begin the swirl stitching, come up in any corner.

2   Place your stitch just under the thread from the previous row by gently moving it out of the way a bit. Make the stitch by going in at the white dot and out at the black dot (right next to the corner of the previous row).

3   Keep a consistent stitch length. For a dense design, make your stitches about 3 mm long (just less than ¼"). A more open swirl also looks nice so experiment with wider stitches. Notice how the needle is always set parallel to the previous row.

Opposite and on this page: Several variations and colorations of swirl designs

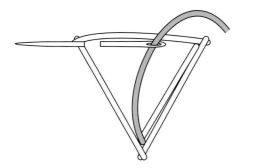

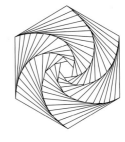

Step 4   Step 5   Complete

4   Take the next stitch to the right, working in a clockwise direction.

5   Continue rotating the ball and stitching until the entire shape is filled.

There are several photographs of swirl stitch on pages 64 and 65, showing just how versatile a single temari design can be. Try different colorations and display them together for wonderful effect. The technique is fairly simple and the balls are quick to make, so they are a great way to experiment with color and stitch placement.

Refine Your Skills Stitch the Swirl in a Counterclockwise Direction

An interesting secondary design appears where two filled shapes meet (both stitched clockwise). You can change this secondary design by alternating shapes filled with swirls stitched in a clockwise direction with those stitched in a counterclockwise direction. Stitch the counterclockwise swirl as shown here.

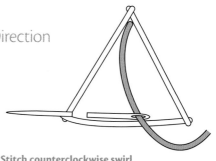

Stitch counterclockwise swirl

Clockwise

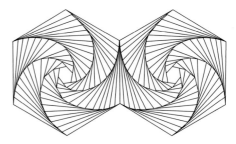

Clockwise (left hexagon) and counterclockwise (right hexagon)

Getting the Right Length of Thread

Wrapped bands can easily be started with your thread still attached to the spool or card (see page 27). Another technique is to measure the right amount of thread by winding it loosely around your ball or by using your paper measuring strip and cutting the thread from the spool. Be sure to add about 6" to 8" for starting and stopping.

Wrapping *(Maki Kagari)*

The three dimensional shape of the temari offers a unique opportunity to design with threads wrapped all the way around the ball. Choose from a variety of wrapped designs, some of which make up quickly and easily and others which combine more advanced techniques like layering and weaving to create very intricate designs.

Wrapped Bands

A wrapped band can be a simple decorative line added around the equator or a more complex design made by wrapping several bands in different

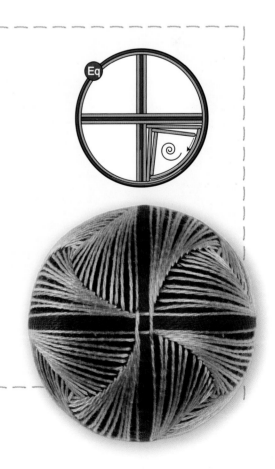

CARIBBEAN SWIRLS PATTERN

25 cm (9 ¾") ball wrapped with black

Sample photographed: Maxi-Lock Black; Vineyard Silk T813 Caribbean (variegated blues) and C134 Lipstick (red)

1 Begin by marking an S4 design with inconspicuous thread, such as sewing thread in a dark color (see page 31).

2 Wrap over the guidelines with a band of thread made up of five rows red bordered by one row variegated blue.

3 Fill each negative space (shaped like a triangle) with swirl stitching using variegated blue thread. Place the stitches for the first row right next to the wrapped bands.

See pages 64 and 65 for more photographs of swirl designs, with different color versions.

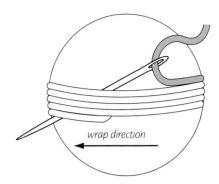

Basic wrapped band

directions and in varying widths. A simple band of threads wrapped around the equator is called an *obi*, after the sash worn at the waist over a kimono, and is often used as a striking accent for simple division temari.

Basic Wrapped Band

A wrapped band is made of one or more rows of thread wrapped straight around the ball. The maximum width of the band depends on the size of the ball; a larger ball can accommodate a wider band without the wraps slipping off the sides. When working with such long lengths of thread, take care to secure the starting thread with a knot or with several stitches taken underground (see Starting Your Thread on page 27). Wrap straight around the ball, laying new rows parallel to previous ones. End off by stitching under the band directly opposite the starting point and coming up on the other side.

On the following pages you will learn some simple techniques for creating special effects on a basic wrapped band temari. Once you become comfortable with wrapping, you will be amazed how fast and easy it becomes!

Opposite: Various wrapped designs, among others

Simple Wrap Along Guidelines

Often, a band is wrapped on both sides of an existing guideline such as the equator on a simple division temari. To begin, come up close to a guideline. Wrap the thread smoothly around the ball, laying it alongside the guideline. Keep turning the ball, laying each row next to the previous one until you have the required number of rows on one side of the guideline. Then stitch underground to the other side of the guideline, complete the remaining wraps, and end off. Try to use the same tension for wrapping the guidelines and for wrapping the threads in the band so they will all lie smoothly together. Try this simple pattern, named Bermuda Reef.

BERMUDA REEF PATTERN
23 cm (9") ball wrapped with yellow

Sample photographed: Maxi-Lock Gold; Kreinik #8 Medium Braid 029 (metallic turquoise) and 51C (metallic blue); Anchor #5 perle cotton: 189 (light turquoise), 187 (medium turquoise), 131 (blue), and 291 (yellow).

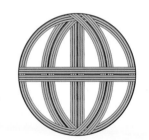

1   Mark an S8 with metallic turquoise (see page 32).

2   Wrap a band on both sides of one vertical guideline (three rows light turquoise on each side). Place the starts for these bands at the equator so that they will be covered in the next step. Then, with medium turquoise, wrap three rows on each side of another vertical guideline. For the remaining vertical guidelines, wrap one row blue on each side.

3   Obi: on each side of the equator, wrap one row yellow and three rows blue. Secure the band with straight stitches made diagonally across (blue metallic).

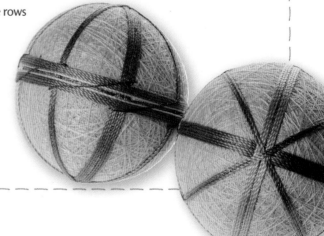

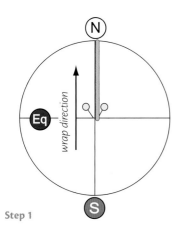

Step 1

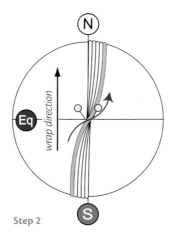

Step 2

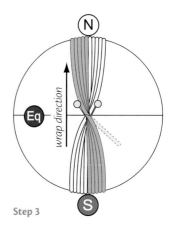

Step 3

Wrapped Bands Using a Pivot Point

Creating a *pivot point* allows you to wrap wider bands on the ball without fear of the thread slipping off the sides. Since there can be quite a buildup of threads at the pivot point, it helps to use a pair of pins, called *keeper pins*, to hold the threads together. To make a wrapped design using pivot points:

1   If you do not already have a reference pin at the equator, place the first keeper pin there. Place a second pin at a slight angle next to it. Come up between two keeper pins (see Starting Your Thread on page 27). Turn the ball as you wrap, laying the thread to the right of the guideline.

2   When you get to the keeper pins on the opposite side of the ball, shift to the other side of the guideline and continue to wrap back to the starting place. Add as many rows as you need, always pivoting to the other side of the guideline at your pivot point between the keeper pins.

3   Continue with the same spool of thread and wrap on the other side of the guideline—to the left of the north pole and to the right of the south pole. As before, always pivot through the keeper pins. Complete all wraps and end off between the keeper pins.

Keeper pins are handy to keep the threads together, but with practice you can wrap without them. You may find that your finished bundles of thread are neater without using keeper pins because you need to pay closer attention to how you lay the thread across the pivot points. If you are neat enough, you can leave the bundles unsecured when the design is finished.

Finishing Off Bundles

When you have finished wrapping the bands, you'll have bundles of thread at each place you had a pivot point. You will need to secure them in some manner. One way is to press them down into the ball and wrap a simple band over them. Another way is to stitch around each individual bundle, taking short underground stitches to get around it if needed. Remove the keeper pins after you have stitched around the bundle.

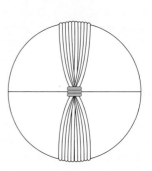

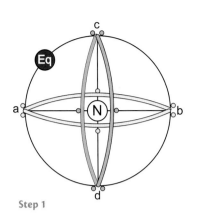

Step 1

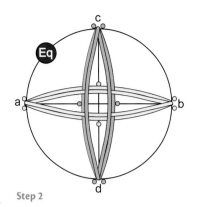

Step 2

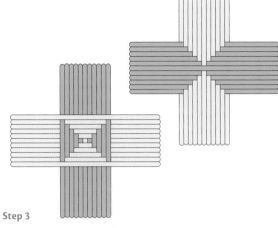

Step 3

Wrapping from the Outside of the Band towards the Inside

This technique is helpful when layering two or more wrapped bands on a ball. Here, you work from the outside of the band making your way toward the center (see page 74 for layering techniques). An interesting design appears where the bands cross.

1 Wrap the outside rows.

2 Add new wraps towards the inside.

3 Continue adding rows until you reach the center. Wrapping one row at a time, from the outside towards the inside, on two layered bands results in the design shown on the right. Beginning in the center and adding new wraps on the outsides of the bands has a totally different look, as shown on the left.

BLUEBERRY PIE PATTERN

25 cm (9³/₈") ball wrapped with dark blue

Sample photographed: Maxi-Lock Navy; Rainbow Gallery Treasure Braid Petite PH13 (metallic copper); Caron Watercolors: 205 (variegated yellows) and 207 (variegated teals)

This pattern is an example of maintaining symmetry with wrapped bands (see page 74).

1 Begin by marking a C10 design with metallic copper (see page 36).

2 Wrap bands of thread, passing through the diamond centers: two rows variegated teals, seven rows variegated yellows, and two rows variegated teals. Weave all bands so they interlock symmetrically.

Alternating Two
Colors on Layered
Wrapped Bands

When wrapping with one color,
temporarily secure the other by
winding it around the keeper pins.

NAUTICAL MOSAIC PATTERN

24 cm (9 3/8") ball wrapped with dark turquoise

Sample photographed: Maxi-Lock Dark Turquoise; Rainbow Gallery
Treasure Braid Petite PB201 (metallic yellow); Finca #5 perle
cotton: 4048 (light turquoise), 4059 (medium turquoise), 1227
(yellow), and 1902 (red)

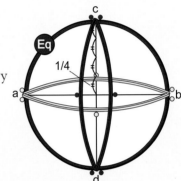

1   Begin by marking an S4 design with medium turquoise (see page 31).

2   Obi: on each side of the equator, wrap one row of your first color (red), two rows of the
second color (light turquoise), and three rows of the third color (yellow).

3   Measure the distance from pole to equator. Places guide pins for the wrapped design on each guideline 1/4
of the distance out from each pole (north and south) for placement of the first row. Place keeper pins next to
the equator pins so you can make wrapped bands with pivot points at the equator.

4   First wrap from direction **a to b** with yellow (two rows wrapped to each side
of north pole and south pole). Lay the thread to the inside of the guide pins.
Then wrap from direction **c to d** with red, laying the thread to the inside
of the guide pins (two rows wrapped to each side of north pole and
south pole). Lay the thread between the keeper pins at the equator.

5   Continue alternating wrapping two rows inward at a time in each
direction. The total number of rows for the wrapped design is as follows.

a to b: ten rows yellow (wrapped two at a time), six rows red
(wrapped two at a time), and two rows medium turquoise.

c to d: ten rows red (wrapped two at a time), six rows yellow
(wrapped two at a time), and two rows medium turquoise.

As with all temari patterns, if your temari is a bit smaller or larger than the
standard ball size or if you used a heavier or lighter thread than usual, you may
need to make adjustments to the total number of rows.

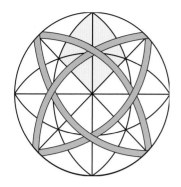
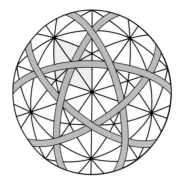
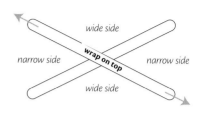

wide side

narrow side   wrap on top   narrow side

wide side

Maintaining Symmetry with Wrapped Bands

Symmetry is an important part of creating attractive temari designs. When wrapping bands on a combination division temari or any other time you wrap multiple bands that cross each other, weave as you wrap to make each intersection look the same. This makes a wrapped design that appears interlocked and outlines new shapes on the ball which you can fill with stitching.

One way to add wraps on a combination division temari is to position the wraps so they run diagonally across the centers of the four-part diamonds (see C8 division on page 33 and combination C10 division on page 36 for help in locating the four-part diamonds).

Begin by coming up in the center of a four-part diamond and wrap straight around the ball, laying the thread over other diamond centers as you go. Complete the number of wraps for the desired width of your first band. To add the second band, come up at a diamond center underneath the first band to hide your start. Lay the thread across the adjacent diamond center to begin wrapping. Make note of the first intersection you just created. It will be shaped like a flattened "X". Look for the wide side and the narrow side and then turn the ball so the intersection is oriented as shown in the diagram.

The band on top will run either from upper left to lower right or from lower left to upper right. Whichever direction is on top is the one you want to maintain as you continue to add new bands. As you come to each intersection, decide if you need to lay the thread on top or weave under the wrapped band already crossing that intersection to maintain the symmetry. Blueberry Pie on page 72 is an example of a pattern in which you will maintain symmetry with wrapped bands.

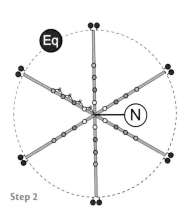

Step 2

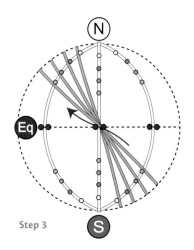

Step 3

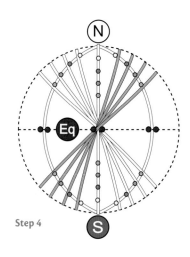

Step 4

Wrapping a Basket Temari

A basket temari is created on a simple division ball by wrapping between pairs of keeper pins placed at the equator. The wraps are separated and spaced equal distances from the poles so an open, uniform grid is created in the center of the design. Try this one on different simple divisions and watch the design in the center change. The technique is very similar to wrapped bands with a pivot point (see page 71).

1   Begin by pin marking a simple division. Wrap the vertical guidelines using the same thread that you select for the center basket design. To keep both pole intersections neat, begin and end the vertical guideline wraps at the equator pins instead of at the north pole. Stitch underground between equator pins to add each new vertical guideline. Do not wrap around the equator but leave the equator guide pins in place.

2   Decide on the spacing between the wraps for the center part of the basket. This will take a little experimenting. The spacing looks nice when the threads are spaced 0.5 to 1 cm ($^3/_{16}$" to $^3/_8$") apart, depending on the size of your temari and the thickness of the thread. For the overall size of your basket, try making it equal to ½ the distance between the pole and the equator. Place guide pins spaced equally out from the pole, along the vertical guidelines on both the north and south pole sides of the ball. Wrap a few times around the ball with your pin layout to check the proportions and then make adjustments to the placement of the pins as you like.

3   Wrap the design by starting between two keeper pins with thread still attached to the spool or skein (see page 27). Place each wrap to the outside of a guide pin (relative to the pole) and lay the thread between the keeper pins (red arrow in the diagram). Leave all pins in place.

Hiding Starts and Stops

It takes some practice to get inconspicuous starts and stops on wrapped bands. Sometimes, portions of your band will be later covered by other stitching. Use this to your advantage; start and end your threads in the area that will be covered later so they won't show on the finished ball.

When wrapping multiple, intersecting bands, begin each new band by coming up under one that is already on the ball. With each new row, stitch under that band. When all rows are complete, end off under it. Your starts and stops will be hidden.

If the starting place cannot be hidden, try to stagger the rows so that starts and stops are not so obvious on the finished design. This is particularly useful when your band is made of multiple colors and you have to change thread color often.

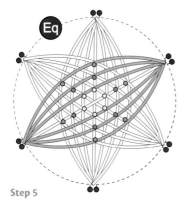

Step 5

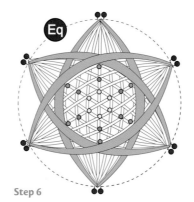

Step 6

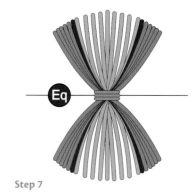

Step 7

4 Continuing with the same spool of thread, pivot between the keeper pins and complete the wraps on the other sides of the poles. End off.

5 Begin again between two keeper pins and follow the same steps for wrapping. Repeat until you have wrapped between each pair of pins.

6 Add a frame around the center basket design by wrapping a band of multiple rows of thread next to the last row of each side of the center basket design.

7 Remove the guide pins from the center part of the basket and adjust threads evenly. Cinch all threads crossing through the keeper pins by stitching around the bundle several times.

There are many variations on the basket design. When you feel confident with the technique, try one of them. For a denser design, make the wraps with two or three threads laying closer together. Try weaving at the center of the basket: wrap in two directions, then, on the third wrap, weave under the first and over the second wraps. A lovely option is to stitch embroidered flowers right on top of the wrapped threads of your basket!

Of course, bring a few temari with you on your next picnic, especially if you have children with you. It is so much fun to toss the balls back and forth to each other! For a larger photograph of Summer Picnic Basket, see page viii.

Summer Picnic Basket Pattern

31 cm (12 ¼") ball wrapped in yellow

Sample photographed: Maxi-Lock Gold (yellow); Finca #5 perle cotton: 4059 (medium teal), 4074 (dark teal), 1902 (red), and 3400 (blue)

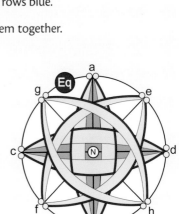

1 Pin mark an S6 (see page 32). Using medium teal, wrap the vertical guidelines for the S6, beginning and ending each one at an equator pin. Do not wrap an equator line but leave the equator pins in place. Position a keeper pin next to each equator pin.

2 Place four pins out from both north and south poles on all guidelines, spacing them 0.7 cm (1/4") apart.

3 Wrap the center basket design with medium teal. Then make the basket frame by wrapping a band next to each side of the center design: one row red and five rows blue.

4 With dark teal, stitch around the threads crossing at the equator to cinch them together.

Little Quilt Square Pattern

23 cm (9") ball wrapped with dark turquoise

Sample photographed: Maxi-Lock Dark Turquoise; Anchor #5 perle cotton: 187 (medium turquoise), 189 (dark turquoise), 298 (yellow), 29 (red), and 131 (blue)

1 Begin by marking an S8 design with medium turquoise (see page 32). Use keeper pins at the equator.

2 Obi: on each side of the equator, wrap seven rows blue and one row yellow.

3 Wrap vertical bands with pivot points at the equator for each vertical guideline, completing the wraps on both sides of a guideline before moving on to the next. The order of wrapping is as follows: a to b (three rows dark teal), c to d (three rows dark teal), a to b (six rows yellow), c to d (six rows yellow), a to b (one row red), c to d (one row red). This completes the first cross. For the second cross, wrap from e to f (six rows yellow and one row red) laying thread just outside the red square created in the first cross. Wrap from g to h (six rows yellow and one row red).

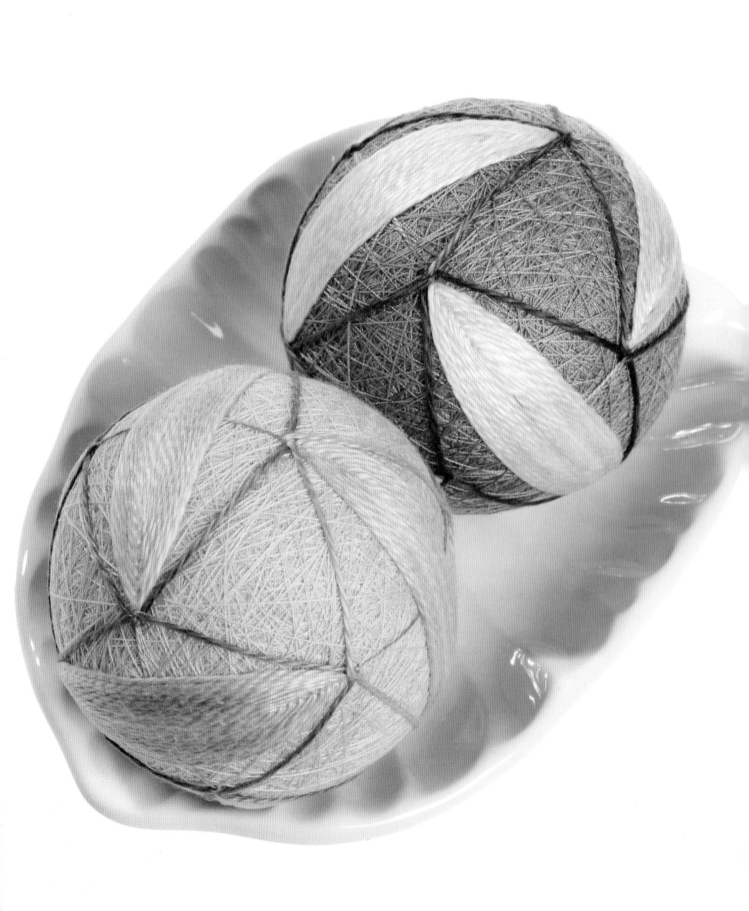

Stitching Simple Shapes

Most of the designs on a temari are made with the same basic stitch, in and out of the thread wrap, taking a small bite into the surface of the ball. This section will get you started using the basic stitch to create polygon shapes such as triangles, squares, and hexagons, as well as a special two-sided shape called the spindle. Along the way, you will discover ways to give your open shape and solid shape designs a well-made and attractive look, such as curving the shape or overlapping threads at the corners. You will also learn two simple but intriguing techniques—interlocking and layering shapes on the same ball. Many of the tips for good stitching techniques presented here are useful for all temari stitching. Master them to create temari designs that are crisp and eye-catching.

Open Shapes

Learn the basic temari stitch by using it to create an open shape like the square (*masu kagari*) on the next page. For many patterns, you will adapt the same technique to make other polygons, such as triangles, hexagons or pentagons. Look through the photographs in the book and see how many open shapes you can quickly identify on the balls shown. You will find that some temari contain multiple shapes, making them all the more interesting to study.

Opposite: Lemon Slices, see page 88

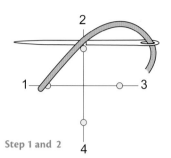

Step 1 and 2

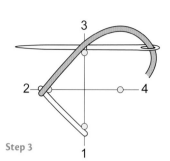

Step 3

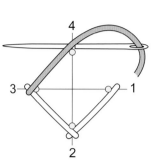

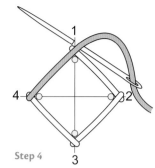

Step 4

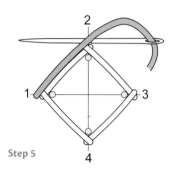

Step 5

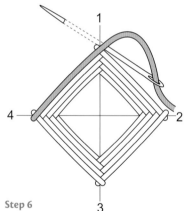

Step 6

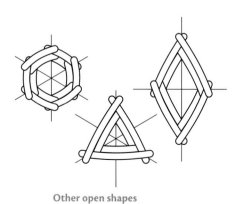

Other open shapes

1 Place guide pins equally spaced from the center along your guidelines so you will know where to place the stitches for the first row. Make an underground stitch, a couple of inches long, and come up to the left of pin 1. (See Starting with a Cut Length of Thread, page 28).

2 Turn the ball counterclockwise and take a stitch at pin 2.

3 Turn the ball counterclockwise and stitch at pin 3. Turn the ball counterclockwise and stitch at pin 4.

4 Place each stitch with your needle perpendicular to the guideline except for the last stitch in a row. Then set your needle at an angle and exit slightly above the first stitch to start row 2.

5 Begin the next row by laying the thread alongside the previous row before making the stitch.

6 Continue stitching around the shape until you have completed the number of rows desired and end off (see Ending Off, page 29).

As you stitch these basic shapes, try to develop a rhythm to your stitching.

- Turn the ball,
- Lay the thread,
- Take the stitch.
- Repeat.

When these motions are repeated consistently and smoothly, you'll relax and your stitching will improve with the practice.

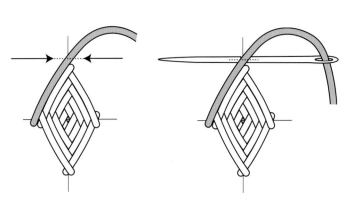

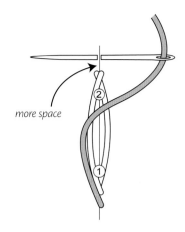

Lay thread in place and stitch

More space between rows

Spacing Between Rows: How Much?

Learning exactly where to place stitches for new rows is always a bit of an experiment. Leave too much space between rows and you will see a gap instead of a solid design. Leave too little space and your threads will bunch up instead of laying flat around the corners. There is an easy technique that works very well to solve this issue: first lay your thread in place alongside the previous row, note where it crosses the guideline and stitch at that spot.

If you decide to stitch without first laying the thread in place, note that the distance between stitches from one row to the next will vary depending on the sharpness of the angle at the corner. As a general rule, the sharper the corner, the larger the distance needed between rows. For instance, you will need to leave less space between the rows on the corner of a square and more space between the rows on the sharp point of a spindle.

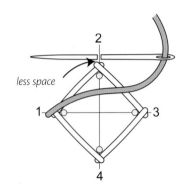

Less space between rows

Refine Your Skills Perfecting the Basic Stitch

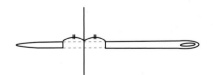

Stitch just deep enough into the thread wrap so that the stitch will stay in place; before pulling the needle through, wiggle it a bit to check for security. Make a short stitch, about 2 mm (1/8") wide, to create a sharp corner on the shape. Position the needle perpendicular to the guideline thread, not at an angle. Enter the ball before the guideline, stitch underneath it, and exit on the other side, while trying to keep the guideline in the middle of the stitch. Try not to catch the guideline thread with your stitch. Keep an eye on your guideline thread to make sure you have not pulled it out of place with the stitch.

Curving Your Shape

When laying your thread on the ball between stitches, it should follow the curve of the ball and create nicely plump shapes. You'll see more of a curve on larger shapes than on smaller ones.

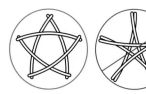

Like this   Not like this

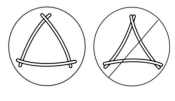

Like this   Not like this

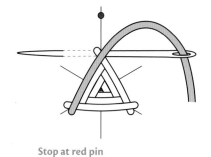

Stop at red pin

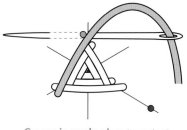

Green pin marks place to restart

Don't Get Lost: Where Do I Stop Stitching?

When you begin stitching the first row of any design, put a red pin on the guideline where you take the first stitch. When you get back to that red pin, you know you have finished a complete row. The red pin is very useful when you stitch a lot of rows and would otherwise lose track of where to place the last stitch to complete the last row.

Where Do I Start Again?

When you need to rethread the needle, you can easily lose your place and not know where to begin again. On which corner of the shape should you restart? This can happen when you run out of thread before completing all the stitching or when you want to change colors within the design. Another little trick with a marking pin will help you remember. Before ending off to re-thread your needle, place a green pin where the needle would have exited the ball if you were not ending off to rethread. Then go ahead and end off by taking an underground stitch that is a couple of inches long in any direction away from your design. Come up and clip the thread close to the surface of the ball. After re-threading the needle, come up at the green pin and continue stitching with the new thread.

Why Keep Track?

Have a look at your square or hexagon or other shape when you've completed all the stitching. Notice how the sides of the shape are all the same length and the angles are the same. Check the way the threads cross over each other at each of the corners on the shape. You should see a symmetrical arrangement where the rows overlap each other one by one. If you look carefully and see a place where the rows look doubled, then that is a spot where you probably lost track of your stitching and added an extra row. Aim for creating stitched shapes that are perfectly symmetrical by keeping track of your stitching.

Variations on Simple Shapes

Practice stitching open shapes on other divisions as follows.

- On an S4, stitch diamonds by placing two points near the pole and the two longer points further from the pole.
- On an S6, stitch open triangles overlapping in the same manner as the squares on Square Dance Pattern (see below).
- On an S10, stitch open pentagons. Any of these can be overlapped, interlocked, or layered (see pages 89 to 92).

The next pattern, Square Dance, is stitched on an S8 division temari. Look at the text on the right for variations on simple shapes like this.

SQUARE DANCE PATTERN

26 cm (10 ¼") ball wrapped in dark blue

Sample photographed: Maxi-Lock Navy; Kreinik #8 Fine Braid 032 (metallic white); DMC #5 perle cotton: 972 (yellow) and 907 (green)

Notice how the sides of the squares bend with the curvature of the ball. As you lay thread for the stitch, try to maintain a consistent curve on each side of the square.

1 Mark an S8 with metallic white (see page 32).

2 Stitch a solid square (five rows green) around the north pole.

3 Measure the distance from pole to equator. Stitch 3 open squares. First square: five rows yellow beginning at a quarter of the distance out from the pole. Second square: five rows green beginning at half of the distance from the pole. Third square: five rows yellow beginning at three quarters of the distance from the pole.

4 Add an open square (one row) on top of each of the squares stitched in Step 3. Stitch on the guidelines not used so that the squares are off-set. Alternate green and yellow thread.

5 Stitch the same design on the south pole side of the ball.

6 Obi: on each side of the equator, wrap seven rows yellow. Stitch a double herringbone (green) over the obi (See page 95).

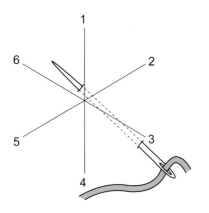

Step 1 Come up left of guideline

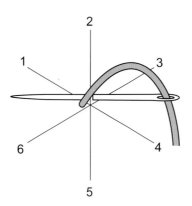

Step 2 Make short stitch

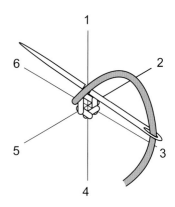

Stitch around each guideline

Solid Shapes

A solid shape is stitched from the center outward. Place the initial stitches very close to the center intersection of guideline threads, leaving only 2 or 3 mm (1/8") of space between the center and your first row of stitches. You should be able to judge this distance by eye instead of placing guide pins for the first row. This small gap will fill in as you complete the first row.

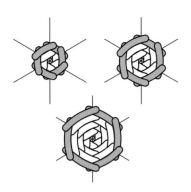

Step 3 Add rows

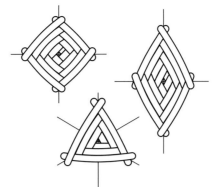

Other solid shapes

Check Your Work with Each Stitch

Practicing these stitching techniques until they become a habit will ease you into creating many more intricate temari designs. Pay attention to each stitch as you progress, training your eye to watch for parallel rows, even tension, symmetrical angles on the shapes, and balanced placement of the entire shape relative to the temari's guidelines.

1 Make an underground stitch, a couple of inches long, and come up to the left of pin 1. (See Starting with a Cut Length of Thread on page 28.)

2 With your needle to the left of the guideline, make a short stitch close to the center intersection.

3 Rotate the ball counterclockwise and stitch around each guideline. Remember to set the needle at an angle to begin each new row.

DAFFODIL PATTERN

24 cm (9 ½") ball wrapped in blue

Sample photographed: Maxi-Lock Chicory (blue); Rainbow Gallery Hi-lights H615 (metallic blue); DMC #5 perle cotton: 4077 (variegated yellow), 972 (orange), and 907 (light green)

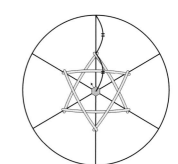

1 Begin by marking an S6 with metallic blue (See page 32).

2 Measure the distance from north pole to equator. Stitch an open triangle beginning half of the distance out from pole. Stitch three rows of variegated yellow and one row of orange. Stitch a similar open triangle on the guidelines not used. You should now have a six-pointed star.

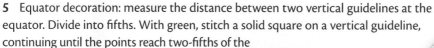

3 With orange, stitch a solid hexagon around the pole. End off when the points reach the triangles stitched in Step 2.

4 Stitch the same design on the south pole.

5 Equator decoration: measure the distance between two vertical guidelines at the equator. Divide into fifths. With green, stitch a solid square on a vertical guideline, continuing until the points reach two-fifths of the distance measured along the equator. Stitch similar solid squares on each of the remaining vertical guidelines. Stitch a double herringbone (one row green), connecting the points of the squares as shown on the diagram.

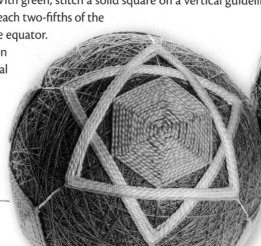

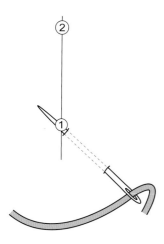
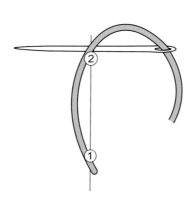
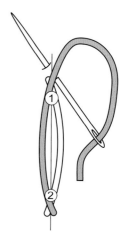

Step 1 Come up at 1

Step 2 Take small stitch under guideline

Step 3 Exit above previous stitch

Spindles (Tsumu Kagari)

A spindle is a simple shape stitched around two points. Mastering this technique requires you to experiment with the amount of tension to apply to each stitch and with the spacing between the stitches. Tension and spacing are important in all temari stitching and especially important for the spindle.

To control the tension, gently lay the thread along the curve of the spindle, smooth it in place, and stitch. When pulling the thread through the ball, hold the stitch in place with your thumb and pull the stitch through the ball keeping it in place without tightening. It will remain in place due to the curvature of the ball and the friction of the thread. Smaller spindles are more difficult to stitch because there is less curvature to the ball on the smaller area.

Learning how much space to leave between the rows on a spindle also requires a bit of practice (see page 81). If you find your stitches bunching up instead of laying neatly to form the spindle shape, you probably need to leave more space between them. This can be several needle widths, depending on the thickness of your thread.

1 Come up at the starting point (to the right and slightly below pin 1).

2 Lay the thread to the left of the vertical guideline. Take a small stitch under the guideline just past pin 2.

3 Turn the ball counterclockwise so pin 1 is at the top. Lay the thread along the left side of the vertical guideline. Set your needle at an angle and exit above the previous stitch to start the next row.

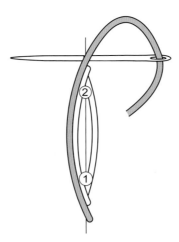

Step 4 Add rows   Complete

4   Continue turning the ball counterclockwise and placing stitches further out from the center so that the spindle gets longer and longer. Leave pins in place until at least three or four rows are complete to keep the spindle from collapsing inward.

LEMON SLICES PATTERN

23 cm (9") ball wrapped in blue (back ball) or bright green (front ball)

Sample photographed on page 78: Back ball—Maxi-Lock Blue; Watercolours by Caron 205 (yellow) and 160 (dark blue); front ball—Maxi-Lock Sour Apple (bright green); Watercolours by Caron 275 (orange-yellow) and 068 (blue-green)

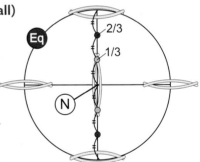

1   Begin by marking an S4 (see page 31) with inconspicuous thread (similar color to the thread wrap) .

2   Your goal is to stitch each of the six yellow spindles on this temari using the same number of rows. Begin with a spindle at the north pole. Measure the distance from pole to equator. Place green guide pins for the starting points of the spindle a third of the distance out from the pole. Place red guide pins for the ending points two-thirds of the distance out from the pole. Stitch the spindle (about ten rows).

3   Using the same thread and the same measurements, stitch a spindle at the south pole. Stitch on the same vertical guidelines as the north pole so the points of the two spindles line up. Try to match the size of your first spindle by stitching the same number of rows.

4   Stitch four spindles at the equator, two placed vertically and two placed horizontally (see diagram). Use the same thread and same measurements as Steps 2 and 3.

5   With dark blue thread, stitch an open diamond (one row) around each spindle so the points of the spindles are connected.

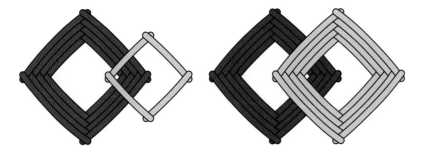

Overlapping squares

Intersecting Shapes

One of the most fascinating aspects of temari is composing a design by experimenting with different arrangements of stitched shapes and the ways that they intersect. There are several methods including overlapping, interlocking, weaving and layering.

Overlapping

Completely stitch the first shape, then stitch the second shape, laying all thread on top of the first shape.

Interlocking (*Nejiri Kagari*)

Create knotted-looking designs by weaving between stitches. Stitch all rows on one shape then begin a second. Weave the threads of the second shape over and under the sides of the first shape as you go. To weave, turn your needle around and slip the eye end under the threads of the first shape. Try not to catch any of the thread wrap. Continue to add rows to the second shape, weaving each row under and over the sides of the first shape like you did for the first row. After completing that shape, you could stitch a third one interlocked with the first two shapes.

Weaving

Do more than just interlock—weave over and under individual threads to create more intricate designs. This is your opportunity to bring techniques from other arts and crafts to temari. Patterns found in woven fabrics, bead weaving, or even chair caning can be recreated on temari at the intersection of two or more bands of thread or stitched shapes. Some of these techniques are described beginning on page 139.

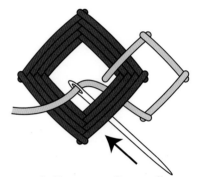

Interlocking squares: Turn needle and slip eye end under threads

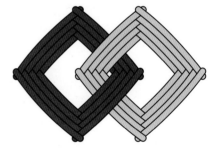

Interlocking squares: Add rows

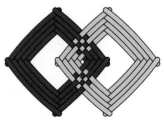

Weaving squares

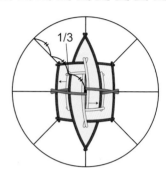

PINWHEEL PATTERN
25 cm (9⁷/₈") ball wrapped in light brown

Sample photographed below (left): Maxi-Lock Mother Goose (light brown); Kreinik #8 Fine Braid 5505 (metallic red); DMC 347 (red), 746 (off-white), 824 (dark blue), and 826 (medium blue)

1 Begin by marking an S8 with metallic red (see page 31).

2 Measure the distance from pole to equator. Stitch an open square beginning a third of the distance down from pole (about 2 cm). Stitch fourteen rows off-white and then one row red.

3 Stitch a spindle (see page 87) interlocked with the square. Begin the spindle just outside the last row of the open square. Stitch fourteen rows medium blue and then one row red.

4 Stitch a second spindle interlocked with the square and the spindle stitched in Step 3. Begin just outside the last row of the square and stitch fourteen rows with dark blue and then one row red.

5 Stitch the same design on the south pole.

6 Obi: on each side of the equator, wrap three rows medium blue.

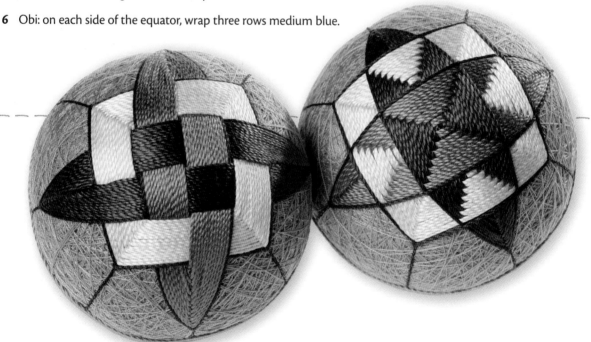

Pinwheel is on the left. The other pattern is Evening Star (see page 93)

Compare Interlocked and Layered Designs

The design for Evening Star looks completely different when the order of stitching is changed and a bit of weaving is included. Pinwheel and Evening Star have the same colors, the same beginning points, and the same number of rows for the three shapes stitched on the temari. The only difference is Pinwheel is interlocked and Evening Star is layered. Experiment with other motifs either by interlocking or layering.

Interlocked motifs

Layered motifs

Layering Kiku Herringbone Designs

To layer two kiku herringbone designs (see page 99), stitch one row on the first shape. Then, when stitching the second, spread open the two stitches that make up an outer point for the first kiku herringbone and stitch around the shared guideline without catching any threads of the stitching threads. Alternate between the two kikus, adding a row at a time on each. Continue to stitch around the shared guideline.

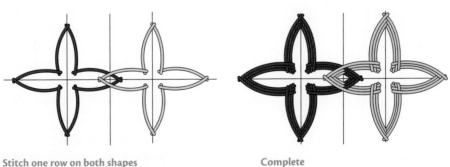

Stitch one row on both shapes   **Complete**

Layer with Multiple Rows

You can create very different looking designs by adding more than one row at a time on each shape. See Raulston Roses (page 134) and Mitsubishi (page 135) for other interesting examples of layered designs.

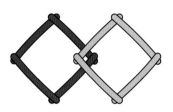
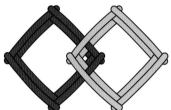

Step 1 Stitch one row on each shape

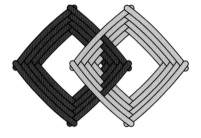

Step 2 Add rows

Layering (*Kousa Kagari*)

A layered design looks very intricate when completed, yet it is easily accomplished by a slight change in the order of stitching.

1   Begin by stitching one row on each of the shapes, overlapping new thread on top of previous stitches without weaving. This is a good time to work with multiple needles, one for each shape.

2   Add another row to each shape. Repeat, adding a new row on each shape until they are the desired size. A secondary design is automatically created where the threads from the shapes cross.

Refine Your Skills Interlocking Three Shapes at a Point

When three or more bands or shapes cross at a single point, you can interlock them by paying careful attention to the over-and-under weaving. Like regular interlocking, complete one element at a time, weaving it with the existing ones.

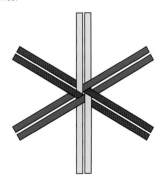

Number the shapes

To create a design that is layered properly, you must stitch the shapes in the same order in each step. Keeping track of the order of stitching becomes a bit of a challenge when you are working with several shapes that intersect. One way to keep track is to write numbers on small pieces of paper and pin one to the center of each shape. With each new step, begin again by adding a row to shape #1 and follow the same order by number.

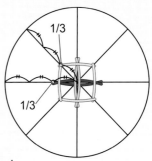

EVENING STAR PATTERN
25 cm (9 ⁷/₈") ball wrapped in light brown
Sample photographed on page 90: Maxi-Lock Mother Goose (light brown); Kreinik #8 Fine Braid 5505 (metallic red); DMC 347 (red), 746 (off-white), 824 (dark blue), and 826 (medium blue)

1 Begin by marking an S8 with metallic red (see page 32).

2 Stitch three layered shapes, adding two rows at a time on each: two spindles and one square. Measure the distance from pole to equator. Begin a dark blue spindle with the first row one third of the distance down from the pole; stitch two rows. Next, stitch another spindle at right angles to the first, using medium blue thread. Place the first row one third of the distance down from the pole. Stitch two rows. Stitch an open square with off-white beginning a third of the distance down from the pole. Place stitches on the lines not used before. Stitch two rows.

   Continue adding two rows at a time on each shape, using the same color and keeping the same stitching order, until the spindles almost fill the open square—about 14 rows. Finish the square by adding the last two rows. Then add one row red around each shape.

3 Stitch the same design on the south pole.

4 Obi: on each side of the equator, wrap three rows medium blue.

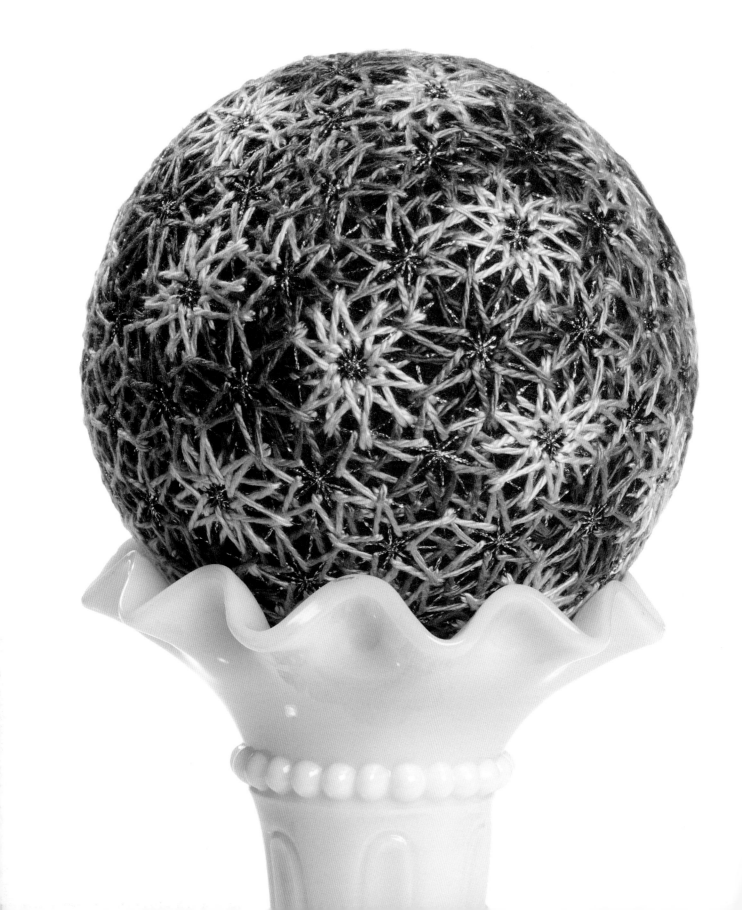

Herringbone Stitches

Herringbone stitch (chidori kagari) is found in the embroidery of diverse cultures around the world from ancient to modern times. While the simple zigzag stitch popular with temari enthusiasts starts out much like the herringbone stitch of surface embroidery, the similarities end as we add multiple rows and alter the stitch placement to create a variety of effects. One of the herringbone variations found exclusively in temari, the kiku herringbone, creates unique and eye-catching flowers in intricately woven circular motifs. These chrysanthemum designs (kiku in Japanese) are the images that often come to mind when the art of temari is mentioned. It's the pattern most people want to make first. Before you jump in, read this chapter from start to finish and decide which variations of herringbone stitch you are using.

Herringbone and Double Herringbone

A common use for the herringbone stitch in temari is to add decoration to an obi wrapped around the equator (*obi kagari*). Using herringbone stitching this way has the added bonus of helping the wraps stay in place.

For stitching over the wrapped obi, choose any thread from the design or use the same thread used for the guidelines. A metallic thread often provides just the perfect sparkle. After you learn *obi kagari* by stitching a herringbone on every guideline, try varying the spacing by skipping over some guidelines. You may have to stitch

Opposite: A hydrangea design using herringbone stitches

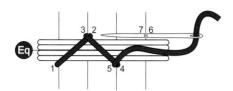

Create sharp point

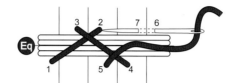

Create open "X"

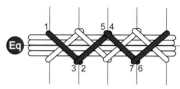

Double herringbone

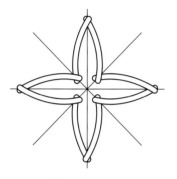

Four-petal flower

Eight-petal flower

more than one time around the ball to complete the path and the results will always be interesting!

To make a single herringbone, make a very short underground stitch (see page 81) to create a sharp point or a longer underground stitch to create a decorative open "X".

Bring your thread up at 1, stitch from 2 to 3, then stitch from 4 to 5, 6 to 7, and so on. Circle your way around the ball and return to your starting point. End off or come up to begin another round as described in the double herringbone stitch below.

A double herringbone stitch is made by making another circuit around the ball but placing your stitches opposite to those from the first row.

In temari, we also have the unique opportunity to make a flower shape with herringbone stitching by placing the stitches closer to the pole rather than over the equator. In the diagrams shown, single herringbone stitch is used to create a four-petal flower and double herringbone stitch is used to create an eight-petal flower.

When herringbone stitching is placed in this way, the stitches nearer the pole are called *inside points*, while those closer to the equator are called *outside points*. Occasionally, you will also see them referred to as top and bottom points.

Refine Your Skills Start Kiku Herringbone at an Inside Point

You can begin each row by coming up at an inside point for the first stitch instead of an outside point. Either method requires you to spot this starting point by eye and you may find one way easier than the other to get consistent looking stitching. Pay attention to your stitch tension to ensure it's the same for this stitch as all the others.

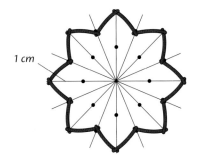

1 cm

Step 1 Place pins and stitch first row

Step 2 Add row

Step 3 Continue adding rows

Net Stitching *(Amime Giku)*

Rows of herringbone stitching, placed with their points overlapping, create the look of a net when stitched on the temari. By utilizing color effectively, you can create a lovely floral motif. Make all your underground stitches short to create sharp points. The more rows and sections you have in the net stitching, the more intricate bloom you will create. When marking a simple division for this stitch, a good rule of thumb is to place the equator pins about 1 cm ($^3/_8$") apart, no matter what size ball you have.

For practice, try marking a 30 cm (11¾") circumference ball into a simple 30 division (S30).

Complete

1   Measure and place pins for stitching one row at a time, beginning with the outer row nearest to the equator and then adding each new row closer to the pole. The spacing of 1 cm ($^3/_8$") between rows yields a pleasing design, but you can make this distance smaller or larger as needed. Stitch the first row with the outside points either at the equator or just above it, depending on how large you would like the finished net design to be. Then add guide pins for the second row, placing them on the same vertical guidelines as the outside points of the previous row and 1 cm ($^3/_8$") closer to the pole from those same outside points.

2   Stitch a row of herringbone with the inside points at the pins. Place stitches at the outside points so they just overlap stitches taken at the inside points of the previous row.

3   Continue adding rows until your last row is close to the center.

Forest Flower Pattern

24 cm (9 ½") ball wrapped in dark red

Sample photographed: Maxi-Lock Red Currant (dark red);
Rainbow Gallery Treasure Braid Petite PB01 (metallic
gold); DMC #5 perle cotton: 369 (light green), 725
(medium yellow), 745 (light yellow), 760 (pink), and 988
(medium green)

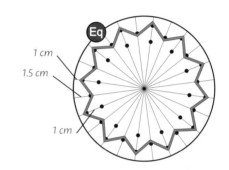

1 Begin by marking an S24 with metallic gold (see page 32).

2 Stitch rows of herringbone to create a net design. Begin with the row nearest the equator. The outside points begin 1 cm (3/8") up from the equator; the inside points begin 1.5 cm (6/8") up from the equator. For the remaining rows, place pins for the inside points by measuring 1 cm (3/8") towards the pole from the outside points of the previous row. Stitch one row medium green, one row light green, one row medium yellow, one row light yellow, one row medium yellow, one row light yellow, one row medium yellow, and two rows pink.

3 Stitch the same net design on the south pole. Make sure to start your points on the same lines used for the north pole design.

4 Obi: on each side of the equator, wrap six rows pink and one row medium green. Stitch a double herringbone over the obi with metallic gold thread.

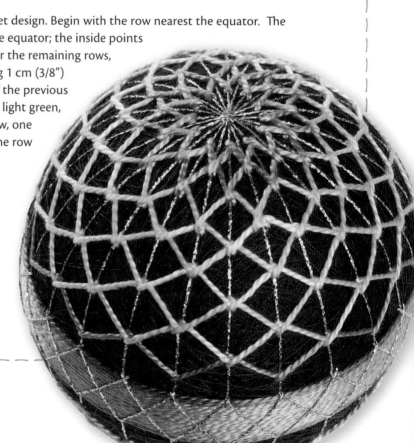

Inside points

Inside points

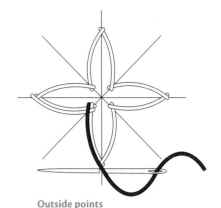

Outside points

Kiku Herringbone (*Uwagake Chidori Kagari*)

This design is named for the chrysanthemum flower (*kiku*), a classic symbol in Japanese culture. The placement of herringbone rows creates beautiful floral effects as well as more abstract and fanciful designs.

Begin by stitching a row of herringbone around the ball, coming up at an outside point to begin the first stitch. In this first row, make all your underground stitches short to make sharp points. Inside points: for all remaining rows, make a longer underground stitch which passes under and around all previous rows. With each new row, the underground portion of the stitch taken at the inside point should be slightly longer in order to travel under and around all previous rows. It should be placed a bit further from the center but close to the previous row.

When several rows are completed, notice that the stitching at the inside point appears to form a woven diamond shape, often called the wedge or cone of the stitch. Outside points: place stitches below the previous row using a short underground stitch to form a sharp point. You may need to leave a small gap between the rows to give the thread room to turn the corner (see Spacing Between the Rows: How much? page 81). Stitching this outside point is very similar to spindle stitching (see page 87).

Kiku herringbone complete

Fill Different Shapes

Fill squares, triangle, diamonds and other shapes with kiku herringbone stitching by varying where you place the first row for the outside points of the design. An easy way to do this is to measure from the outside border of the shape you are filling toward the center and place pins equal distances from that border in order to stitch the first row.

Clematis Bloom (right); Dusty Rose (center); Jasmine (left)

CLEMATIS BLOOM PATTERN

31 cm (12 ¼") ball wrapped in off-white

Sample photographed opposite (right): Maxi-Lock Eggshell (off-white); Rainbow Gallery Nordic Gold ND2 (metallic gold); Vineyard Silk: C-065 (light green), C-162 (off-white), C-122 (pink), and C-179 (medium green)

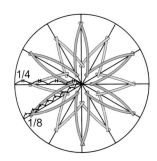

1 Begin by marking an S12 with metallic gold (see page 32).

2 Stitch a kiku herringbone around the north pole. Measure the distance from pole to equator. Begin the inside points a quarter of the distance down from the north pole; begin the outside points a quarter of the distance up from the equator. Stitch three rows off-white, five rows light green, and seven rows medium green (or until the outside points reach the equator).

3 Move over one guideline and stitch a kiku herringbone, overlapping all rows on top of the Step 2 stitching. Divide the pole to equator distance into eight equal segments. Begin the inside points an eighth of the distance down from the pole; begin the outside points an eighth of the distance up from the equator. Stitch seven rows pink or until outside points reach the equator.

4 With yellow, stitch two rows around the pole, right next to the center intersection of guidelines.

5 Stitch the same design on the south pole.

DUSTY ROSE PATTERN

25 cm (9 ¾") ball wrapped in medium pink

Sample photographed opposite (center): Coats and Clark 210-158 (medium pink); DMC #8 perle cotton 760 (medium pink); DMC #5 perle cotton: 818 (light pink) and 3328 (dark pink)

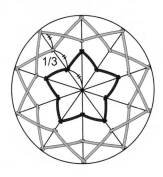

1 Begin by marking an S10 (see page 32) with pink perle cotton #8 (matches thread wrap).

2 Stitch a reverse kiku herringbone (see next page) just above the equator on the north pole side of the ball. Measure the distance from pole to equator. Begin the outside points at the equator and begin the inside points a third of the distance up from the equator. Stitch five rows light pink and one row dark pink. Move over one guideline and stitch the same design, overlapping all rows on top of the first one.

3 Stitch a smaller reverse kiku herringbone inside the one stitched in Step 2. The outside points begin next to Step 2 stitching. The inside points begin a third of the distance down from the pole. Stitch two rows dark pink and five rows light pink.

4 Add lazy daisy stitches (page 59) between each guideline next to the pole, alternating light pink and dark pink. Stitch lazy daisy stitches (one around another) next to the design stitched in Step 3 (see photo for placement).

5 Stitch the same design on the south pole.

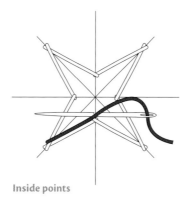

Inside points   Outside points

Reverse Kiku Herringbone (*Sakasa Uwagake Chidori Kagari*)

Work from the outside of the design towards the center to create this topsy turvy motif.

Inside points: make your underground stitches at the inside points short for a sharp point and place each new row closer to the center.

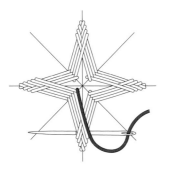

Lengthen underground stitch

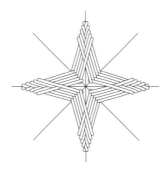

Reverse kiku herringbone

Outside points: underground stitches at the outside points are taken under and around all previous rows and are placed a bit closer to the center than the previous row. With each new row, make the underground stitch a bit longer to encompass the previous rows.

CLASSIC KIKU PATTERN

31 cm (12 ¼") ball wrapped in beige

Sample photographed opposite (right): Isacord 1140 (beige); Rainbow Gallery Nordic Gold ND2 (metallic gold); DMC #5 perle cotton: 369 (light green), 988 (medium green), 987 (dark green), 725 (yellow), 760 (light pink), 3328 (medium pink), 815 (dark pink), and 347 (dark red)

1 Begin by marking an S16 with metallic gold (see page 32).

2 Obi: on each side of the equator, wrap three rows light green, three rows medium green, and three rows dark green. With gold metallic, stitch a double herringbone over the obi.

3 Stitch a layered, kiku herringbone design on the north pole. Layer the stitching by working one row at a time on alternating guidelines. (See Layering, page 92) Measure the distance from pole to equator. The inside points begin 0.5 cm (3/16") down from the pole and the outside points begin a third of the distance up from the equator. This is a good time to use a 0.5 cm paper circle guide (see page 13) pinned to the pole for stitching the inside points. Stitch two rows yellow, two rows light pink, three rows medium pink, two rows dark pink, one row dark red, and one row metallic gold for each layer.

4 Stitch the same design on the south pole.

RED DAHLIA PATTERN

26 cm (10 ¼") ball wrapped in brown

Sample photographed opposite (left): Maxi-Lock Brown; Kreinik #8 Fine Braid 008 (metallic green); DMC #5 perle cotton: 760 (pink), 3328 (light red), 347 (medium red), 815 (dark red), 725 (yellow), and 988 (green)

1 Begin by marking an S12 with metallic green (see page 32).

2 Using metallic green, stitch one row around the north pole, close to the center, to create a solid center for the flower.

3 Stitch a layered, descending herringbone around the north pole. Layer the stitching by working one row at a time on alternating guidelines (see Layering, page 92). Begin the inside points right next to the green stitching done in Step 2. Measure the distance from pole to equator. Begin the outside points half the distance down from the pole. Stitch a total of two rows pink, two rows light red, two rows medium red, one row dark red, one row yellow, and one row green.

4 Stitch yellow French knots around the center, next to the metallic green stitching.

5 Stitch the same design on the south pole.

6 Obi: on each side of the equator wrap one row yellow, two rows dark red, two rows medium red, and two rows light red.

7 With green thread, stitch a double herringbone over the obi. Place your stitches at the outside points of the flowers on each pole.

Stitch with Doubled Thread

Sometimes you'll want a denser look to your ribbed kiku motif. Try using two strands of thread in the needle at a time. When you stitch around the previous row at the inside point, don't forget that it includes two threads.

Ribbed Kiku Herringbone *(Sujidagiku Kagari)*

This variation of the kiku herringbone requires you to focus on tension and careful placement of the stitches at the inside points to create a ribbed or braided look. Loosen your tension so that the rows nest together rather than pulling apart and creating gaps. This stitch and the descending herringbone stitch (page 106) have the nice design bonus of creating a wide design that covers much of the ball.

Classic Kiku (right); Red Dahlia (left)

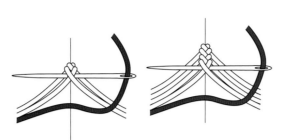

Inside points

Ribbed kiku herringbone complete

Stitch the first two rows with regular kiku herringbone (page 99). Inside points: when stitching at the inside point for the third row, gently move the second row stitch down a bit so you can take the stitch around only the second row. Place this stitch as close as you can to the first row stitch. Then nudge the second row stitch back in place and continue. With each new row, stitch only around the previous row. Outside points: the outside points are made with a short underground stitch just the same as a kiku herringbone.

Descending Herringbone *(Shitagake Chidori Kagari)*

Rows of single herringbone nested closely together form a solid design perfect for depicting a flower with many petals. The floral effect is more pronounced when you layer two motifs on alternate guidelines.

Refine Your Skills Changing Color Within a Design

This little trick can be done while stitching any temari. It is especially effective when stitching kiku herringbone designs. Begin stitching with one color and then change colors partway through so that the points are stitched in different colors. When changing threads, you can either end off and start the new thread or you can stitch underground, coming up at the point where that color will begin on the next row. See the temari photographed on page 103—the rightmost ball on the second row. Imagine this temari in Christmas colors—it makes a wonderful holiday ornament. Wrap the ball with black thread and mark with C8 guidelines. Fill each eight-part square with emerald and dark pink kiku herringbone designs.

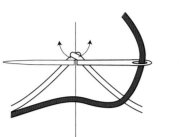

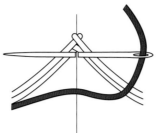

Inside points

Descending herringbone complete

Begin by bringing the thread up at an outside point. Stitch one row of herringbone using short underground stitches to make sharp points. End that row and come up to begin the second row at an outside point just below the first row. Inside points: place your stitches at the inside points further from the center, under the previous row, and very close together by moving the previous row up and out of the way a bit. Stitch as close as possible to the previous row. After taking a stitch, move the previous row back in place. Outside points: make these with a short underground stitch just the same as a regular kiku herringbone.

JASMINE PATTERN
29cm (11³/₈") ball wrapped in yellow

Sample photographed on page 100: Maxi-Lock Sunshine (yellow); Rainbow Gallery Treasure Braid Petite PB201 (metallic yellow); Royal Fashion Crochet Thread Size 3: 0264 (green) and 0423 (yellow)

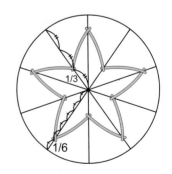

1 Begin by marking an S10 with metallic yellow (see page 32). Wrap the vertical guidelines only, not the equator. Tack the vertical guidelines at the equator pins.

2 Stitch a ribbed kiku herringbone around the north pole. Measure the distance from pole to equator. Begin the inside points a third of the distance down from the pole and begin the outside points a sixth of the distance up from the equator. Stitch two rows green; then alternate stitching one row yellow and one row green for a total of 14 rows. The outside points will extend beyond the equator by several rows.

3 Stitch the same design on the south pole. Place stitches for the inside points on the guidelines used for the outside points on the north pole motif.

More Stitching Techniques

The techniques in this chapter expand upon those you have already learned. As you become more and more familiar with the basics and start mastering more challenging techniques, you will begin to see how you can combine multiple patterns on the same ball to create designs that are truly unique. In this chapter, you'll begin with stitching techniques that encircle the ball and move on to intricate and exciting continuous paths designs. As you read, be sure to study the photographs of these rather complex temari so that you completely understand how they are constructed. You will then be ready to try the challenge designs in the following chapter.

Merry-Go-Round Stitching *(Jyouge Douji Kagari)*

"Up-and-down-at-the-same-time-stitching" is the direct translation from Japanese for this fun, beginner technique. Also called pole-to-pole or north-south concurrent stitching, it is worked on a simple division temari by alternating stitching between the northern and southern hemispheres. Between stitches, spin the ball and lay the thread over the equator. Keeping the north pole oriented to the top as you work will result in threads ordered correctly.

Opposite: A bowlful of challenging designs

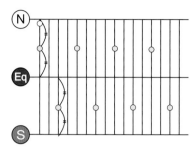

Step 1 Pin placement

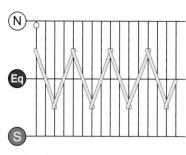

Step 2

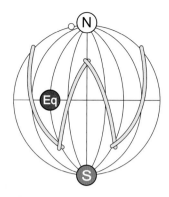

Alternate view

The first row is a basic herringbone (see page 95), making a wave of up-and-down stitching all the way around the ball and returning to the starting point. With the second row, select from the variety of herringbone variations—any of them will work. You can create a pivot point (see page 71) at the equator or not, depending on your choice of stitches and design ideas. Using keeper pins (see page 71) at the pivot point on the equator is a good idea if you will be stitching many rows. For a classic, symmetrical temari design, create a pivot point at the equator and use the same type of stitch in each hemisphere. Complete the number of rows desired for the first path (the wave of up-and-down stitching) and then stitch the same design with the points reflected as a second path (see Classic Merry-Go-Round, page 111).

Successful completion of this technique helps the beginning stitcher jump from stitching a motif in one small area of the temari to understanding how to create a design around the entire ball. It's an important concept to learn before moving from simple divisions to combination divisions.

Merry-Go-Round Variations

Look carefully a the photographs on pages 111 to 114 to see how interesting and varied merry-go-round designs can be. Some of the techniques that follow involve using different stitches in each hemisphere to vary your merry-go-round design. Others involve varying the placement of stitches along the vertical guideline. You can also lay the thread between the vertical guidelines when you cross the equator.

Follow these simple steps to make the basic merry-go-round path.

1 Pin mark the path for the first row by deciding where to stitch along the vertical guideline (halfway point between pole and equator in the diagram) and how many vertical guidelines to skip over (just one in the diagram). Place a white pin on this guideline near the north pole so you

will remember the location of the starting point when stitching
multiple rows. This will also remind you to keep this side of the ball
oriented upwards while stitching.

2 Bring the thread up to begin stitching in the northern hemisphere.
Aim for the southern hemisphere: lay the thread over the intersection of
the equator and the vertical guideline to the right. Take a stitch at the pin
in the southern hemisphere.

CLASSIC MERRY-GO-ROUND PATTERN
28 cm (11") ball wrapped with turquoise
Sample photographed: Maxi-Lock Dark Turquoise; DMC #8 perle cotton
437 (tan); DMC #5 perle cotton: 433 (brown), 598 (blue), and 746 (off white).
Mark an S16 with tan #8 perle cotton

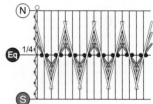

1 Begin by marking an S16 with tan #8 perle cotton (see page 32).

2 Stitch the first path (the wave of up-and-down stitching): measure the distance
from equator to pole and divide into fourths. Place pins for the first color (brown)
at a quarter of this distance above and below the equator. Skip over one vertical
guideline between stitches. Stitch three rows brown using a basic herringbone stitch
and building towards the poles. The diagram shows just one row for clarity. Place pins
for the second color (blue) at half the distance from equator to pole and stitch using
the same method (three rows blue). Place pins for the third color (off-white) at three quarters of the
distance from equator to pole and stitch using the same method (3 rows off-white).

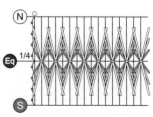

3 Stitch the second path (the wave of up-and-down stitching): repeat Step 2 with the points reflected.

4 Stitch around the bundles of thread at the equator with blue.

A selection of merry-go-round temari

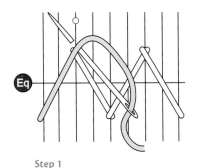

Step 1

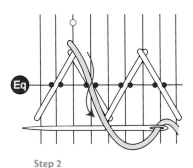

Step 2

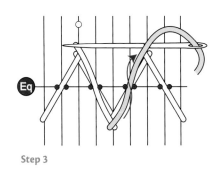

Step 3

3 Aim for the northern hemisphere: lay the thread over the intersection of the equator and the next vertical guideline to the right. Take a stitch at the pin in the northern hemisphere. Repeat, stitching a zig zag path until you return to your starting point.

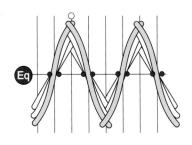

Step 4

Easy Variation

For the easiest of all versions of the technique, try this.

1 Begin by stitching the first row close to the equator and add basic herringbone stitches for new rows on the pole sides of the vertical guidelines. After stitching the first basic herringbone row, enter the ball to complete that row, set the needle at an angle, and exit to the left of the vertical guideline to begin the second row.

2 Aim for the south pole: lay your thread to the right of the first row, through the keeper pins, pivot across the equator, and lay the thread to the left of the first row. Make the stitch on the south pole side of the first row.

3 Aim for the north pole: lay your thread to the right of the first row, through the keeper pins, pivot across the equator, and lay the thread to the left of the first row. Make the stitch on the north pole side of the first row.

4 Continue until you reach your starting point. Add more rows as desired, always pivoting at the equator and making new stitches on the pole side of the previous row.

MERRY-GO-ROUND WITH KIKU HERRINGBONE PATTERN

28 cm (11") ball wrapped in turquoise

Sample photographed: Maxi-Lock Brown, marked with DMC #8 perle cotton (blue), and stitched with DMC #5 perle cotton: 437 (brown), 4025 (variegated turquoise), and 746 (off-white)

Follow the same steps as for the Classic Merry-Go-Round (on page 111) but use a different stitch—a kiku herringbone (see page 99), as follows.

1 Begin the first row close to the poles and work towards the equator. Stitch the first row then set your needle at an angle to end the first row and begin the second.

2 Aim for the southern hemisphere: lay the thread to the left of the first row, pivot at the equator, and lay the thread to the right of the first row. Stitch under and around the first row, placing the stitch nearer the equator.

3 Aim for the northern hemisphere: lay the thread to the left of the first row, pivot at the equator, and lay the thread to the right of the first row. Stitch under and around the first row, placing the stitch nearer the equator.

4 Continue adding new rows by working towards the equator.

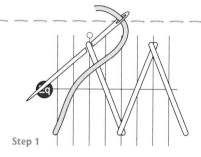
Step 1

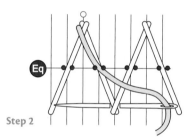
Step 2

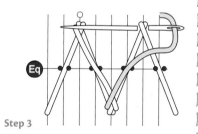
Step 3

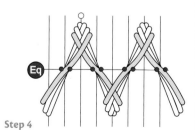
Step 4

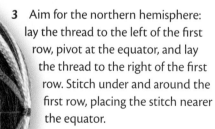

Stitch a Solid Star

To create a solid star (with the center completely filled in), you will need to begin with your points close to the center, about 0.5 cm (3/16") when you use a #5 perle sized fiber for stitching. The first row will close in and cover the center. Add new rows around the outside to make the star bigger and bigger.

Continuous Motifs *(Hito Hude Gake)*

Do you remember drawing stars in elementary school? You put your pencil on the paper, draw five straight lines along a path without lifting the pencil, and end right back where you started with a five-point star. You can stitch a star on temari in much the same way by taking a basic stitch at each turn your pencil would make. You are not limited to stars, though; there are many other continuous motifs which can be created in the same manner. These are different than the ones created when learning the basic stitch (page 81) because the thread path will cross over other stitches in the same motif as you stitch.

The Japanese have a phrase, *hito hude gake* (one stroke of the brush), to describe a kanji character that can be drawn with a single stroke of the calligraphy brush. Temari artists have borrowed this phrase to describe these continuous paths where one single stitching path will create the entire figure. Some motifs have special names because they are so common: *hoshi kagari* (five-point star) and *mitsubane kikkou kagari* (tri-wing). After exploring the individual *hito hude gake* motifs, try the "one stroke" technique to complete multiple motifs with just one stitching path. Setting up the path is an intriguing temari puzzle; stitching along the path is a relaxing, almost meditative, experience.

Practice by drawing the path for your first continuous motif on paper to get a feel for how it is created. You could also place pins in your temari and wind perle cotton along the path to visualize the completed motif. Typically, diagrams will have the stitches numbered to help you get started. You can pin numbered slips of paper to the guidelines on the ball to help you stitch the first row.

Continuous motif temari

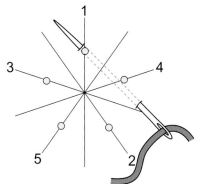

Begin at pin1

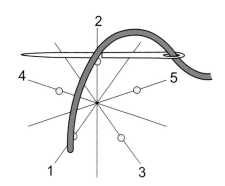

Stitch at pin 2

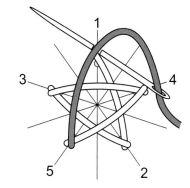

Last stitch at pin 1

Add rows

Five-Point Star (Hoshi Kagari)

Stitch this star along a single path, just as you would draw a star on paper. To make this open star, bring thread up at the pin on line 1 to the left of the guideline. Rotate the ball counterclockwise and stitch at each of the numbered lines in order. When you get back to line 1, set your needle at an angle to end the first row and begin the second.

PEARL STAR PATTERN

24 cm (9 ³/₈") ball wrapped in lavender

Sample photographed: Maxi-Lock Orchid (lavender); Rainbow Gallery Silk Lame Braid SL03 (cream); Anchor #5 perle 110 (lavender) and 926 (off-white)

1 Begin by marking an S10 with cream silk lame braid (see page 32).

2 Inner star: stitch a solid five-point star beginning about 0.5 cm (3/16") from the pole with off-white perle cotton. Add rows until the star points reach half of the distance from pole to equator (about fifteen rows).

3 Outer star: begin quarter way up from the equator on the same lines as the inner star. Lay the thread next to the tips of the inner star. Stitch two rows off-white perle, one row cream silk lame, and one row lavender perle.

4 Finish the inner star by adding new rows just over the sides of the outer star: two rows cream silk lame and one row lavender perle.

5 Stitch the same design on the south pole.

6 Obi: on each side of the equator, wrap five rows off-white perle, one row cream silk lame, and one row lavender perle. With cream silk lame, stitch a double herringbone over the obi.

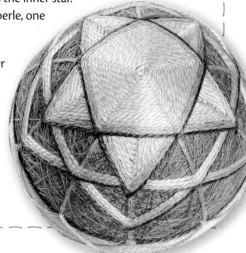

Tri-wing *(Mitsubane Kikkou Kagari)*

This little puzzle is a common continuous motif found in temari. Its Japanese name means "three wings or feathers and tortoise shell shape." The feathers are arranged with their points touching like those on the end of an arrow. A tortoise shell is symbolized by the hexagon shape in the center. This motif is also called a *trefoil*.

A tri-wing is stitched using three equally spaced guidelines. You will place two stitches on each of these guidelines: one stitch for an outside point and one stitch for an inside point. It helps to place a pin on each of these three guidelines to identify them. Ignore the other guidelines by laying your thread over them between stitches. Outside points: use pins equally spaced from the center to mark the first row for the outside points. Inside points: to create a solid tri-wing, place the first row of inside points very close to the center.

Follow the steps on the next page to learn how to stitch a basic tri-wing. This is a skill you will use for many captivating temari designs.

Iris (back), Whirly Bird (front); Mariposa Lily (left)

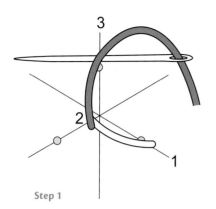

Step 1

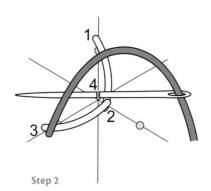

Step 2

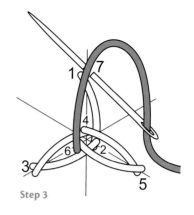

Step 3

1 Bring the thread up for stitch 1 at an outside point. Rotate the ball counterclockwise and make stitch 2 for an inside point. Rotate the ball counterclockwise and make stitch 3 for an outside point.

2 Continue to rotate the ball and alternate stitching at inside and outside points.

3 When you return to the starting point, set your needle at an angle and exit to start the next row or to end the thread.

4 Add new rows around the outside to make the tri-wing bigger, layering new rows on top of the previous ones where they cross. When stitching at the inside points, spread open the two parts of the "wing" a bit so you have room to stitch around the guideline without catching any of the yellow thread. Groom the "wings" when you are done to nudge all the threads towards the guidelines. Tri-wings do not naturally form a

Refine Your Skills Interlocked Continuous Motifs

You can weave between stitches to create motifs that appear knotted. (See Interlocking, page 89).
Establish the over-and-under pattern on your first row, checking it carefully before adding more rows.

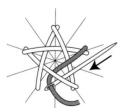 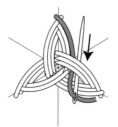 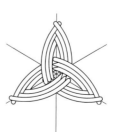 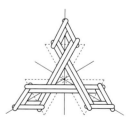

Interlocked Continuous Motifs

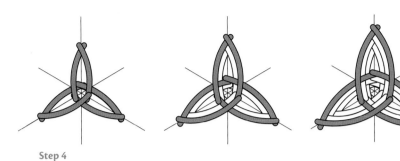

Step 4

regular hexagon at their center so with each new row, take care to adjust the shape of the hexagon forming in the middle so all sides are even. Just exaggerate the curve of the thread a bit until the shape looks even to you. Bigger tri-wings require more adjustment.

While stitching the Mariposa Lily Pattern below, you learned that the tri-wing is stitched on three guidelines. Without doing any weaving

MARIPOSA LILY PATTERN

24 cm (9 3/8") ball wrapped in off-white.

Sample photographed on page 117: Maxi-Lock Eggshell (off-white); Kreinik #8 Fine Braid 015 (fine metallic green) and #16 Medium Braid 015 (medium metallic green); Anchor #5 perle cotton: 96 (light violet), 89 (dark plum), and 98 (medium violet)

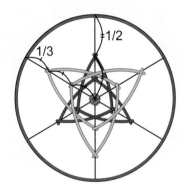

1   Begin by marking an S6 with fine metallic green (see page 32).

2   With light violet, stitch a solid hexagon at the north pole (five rows).

3   Stitch a tri-wing around the hexagon. Measure the distance from pole to equator. Inside points begin next to the hexagon; outside points begin half of the distance down from pole. Stitch two rows dark plum, five rows medium violet, and one row medium metallic green.

4   With medium metallic green, stitch a tri-wing (one row) on the guidelines not used before, with outside points beginning a third of the distance up from the equator and inside points beginning about 0.5 cm (3/16") from the tri-wing stitched in Step 3.

5   Stitch the same design on the south pole of the ball.

6   Obi: on each side of the equator, wrap one row dark plum and five rows light violet. With fine metallic green, stitch a double herringbone over the obi with stitches at each guideline.

More Continuous Motifs

So far, this section has focused on two continuous motifs, the five-point star and the tri-wing. Yet continuous motifs can be stitched in myriad ways. You can trace them in temari designs you see in other places or create your own. Try drawing them on paper first, planning support lines if necessary.

Below are a few diagrams to get you started. Use them as large motifs on a simple division temari or as smaller repeated motifs on combination divisions. Count the number of guidelines necessary to determine which marking to use.

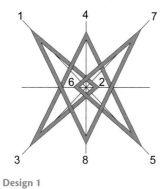

Design 1

Design 2

Design 3

Design 4

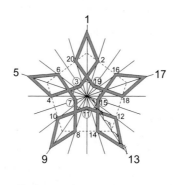

Design 5

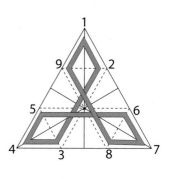

Design 6

(passing your needle and thread over and under previous stitches), this continuous motif has the threads built up in layers. As you add more stitches to Mariposa Lily, you see a hexagon automatically form in the center of the design. Next, try the interlocked version of the tri-wing with Whirly Bird. After taking a stitch at an outside point on the tri-wing, weave under the leg of the adjacent wing, then stitch at an inside point. See Interlocked Continuous Motifs (page 118).

WHIRLY BIRD PATTERN
24 cm (9 3/8") ball wrapped in off-white.
Sample photographed on page 117 (front): Maxi-Lock Eggshell (off-white); YLI Candlelight Metallic Yarn 025 (metallic green) and 012 (metallic lavender); Anchor #5 perle cotton 255 (green) and 110 (purple)

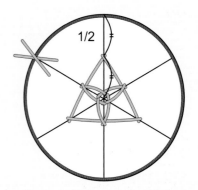

1   Begin by marking an S6 with metallic green (see page 32).

2   Measure the distance from pole to equator. With green perle cotton, stitch an open triangle (one row) with the points beginning half of the distance down from the pole. On alternate guidelines, stitch an interlocked tri-wing with green perle cotton (one row). Inside points begin near the pole and outside points begin just outside the triangle. Continue to alternate stitching between triangle and tri-wing, stitching one row on each at a time. When stitching the triangle, lay the thread to the outside of the tri-wing points, creating a small gap between the rows of the triangle. Total row count for the triangle is five rows green. Total row count for the interlocked tri-wing is two rows green, seven rows dark lavender, and one row metallic lavender.

3   With metallic lavender, stitch a hexagon connecting the points of triangle and tri-wing.

4   Stitch the same design on the south pole.

5   Obi: on each side of equator, wrap four rows dark lavender perle and one row green perle. Stitch large cross stitches over obi at the guidelines with green perle. Use metallic lavender to stitch straight stitches vertically over obi at each guideline and halfway in between.

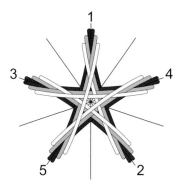

Adding rows toward center

Inward Stitching on Continuous Motifs (Sakasa Kagari)

Many of the stitching variations discussed in the section on herringbone stitches (see pages 95 to 107) can be applied to continuous motifs. With a minor change in stitch placement, your shape can have a completely different look. The inward stitching variation is a particularly nice choice.

Just like inward stitching on other shapes, you can stitch continuous motifs by adding rows towards the center. First, stitch a large open shape and lay the thread in a gentle curve toward the center intersection of guideline threads (instead of towards the outside). When adding more rows, take stitches under and all around previous rows. Between stitches, lay thread alongside the previous row and on the side toward the center. Continue until your stitching fills the entire shape. In these drawings, row 1 is purple, row 2 is green, and row 3 is cream colored.

Refine Your Skills Open Continuous Motifs

Continuous motifs can be stitched with a solid center by beginning close to the shape's center or they can be stitched leaving the center open. Simply extend the points so that the first row does not lie so close to the center of the shape. For added design interest, the center can be filled in with a solid basic shape. This will give you the look of a solid continuous motif but without extra rows on the outside points. In the case of a tri-wing, stitching a regular hexagon center first can help to keep a regular hexagon shape to the tri-wing center.

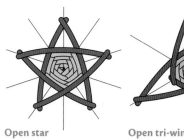

Open star   Open tri-wing and hexagon

Hot Pink Star Pattern
22 cm (8 ⅝") ball wrapped in off-white

Sample photographed: Maxi-Lock Navy; Rainbow Gallery Treasure Braid Petite PB03 (metallic gold); Anchor #5 perle cotton: 89 (medium pink), 298 (yellow), 87 (light pink), and 255 (green)

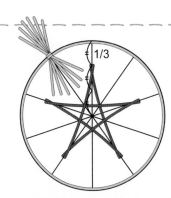

1 Begin by marking an S10 with metallic gold (see page 32).

2 Measure the distance from pole to equator. Stitch a five-point star in an inward direction with points beginning a third of the distance up from equator: seven rows medium pink, one row yellow, and two rows light pink.

3 Stitch the same design on the south pole.

4 Obi: on each side of equator, wrap two rows green, three rows light pink, and two rows medium pink.

5 With green, stitch large pine needle designs over the obi. Tack threads at the centers of the pine needle designs together with two green stitches.

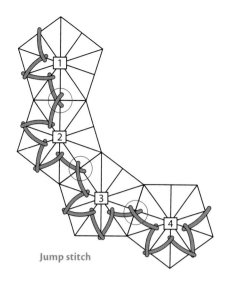

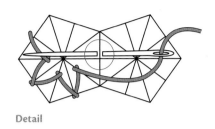

Jump stitch   Detail

Completing Multiple Motifs in One Hito Hude Gake *Stitching Path*

This extraordinary technique uses a single, continuous path to complete not just one, but several motifs located in adjacent shapes. Learn the technique by stitching half of your path in one color and the remaining portion in a second color. Once you are familiar with this expansion of the "one stroke" path for more than one motif, you can stitch the entire design with a single color scheme and save thread and time. When motifs are stitched so their points cross outside the lines of the shape, you'll need to overlap, interlock, or layer those points. The method of pinning a numbered slip of paper to the center of each shape for proper layering (see page 92) can be avoided by first working out the *hito hude gake* path.

Combined with Layered Kiku Herringbone The most

common use of the *hito hude gake* technique is to create layered kiku herringbone motifs (see page 91), with one design placed in each shape on the ball. Try this first before moving on to more advanced designs using other stitches.

Begin by marking your path. Place a numbered slip of paper in the center of each shape. As you work your way along the path, stitch only a portion of the motif within a shape, then jump to the adjacent shape across their shared guideline. When you reach the end of the numbered path, complete that entire motif and work your way back to the beginning. Leave the numbered slips in paper in place until you have learned the path. They can then be removed.

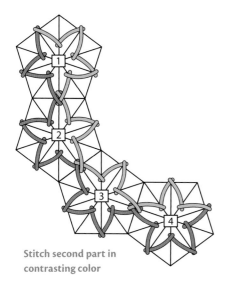

Stitch second part in
contrasting color

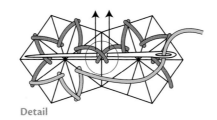

Detail

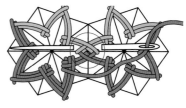

Add new rows

Change thread color in the last shape along your path and stitch
back to the starting point with the contrasting color. You'll be able to
easily see how each motif is made in two parts. Always place the jump
stitches inside the kiku petals by gently moving the previous stitches
out of the way.

With each new row, make the underground portion of the jump
stitch a bit longer. Try to match the spacing between rows to the points
created without jump stitches. When finished, you should not be able
to tell the difference between the two other than the color change.

Complete

Refine Your Skills *Hito Hude Gake* Variations

Try setting up a *hito hude gake* path through any group of shapes.
You can fill the squares and hexagons on a 14-faces marking
(page 49) using a *hito hude gake* path. Another option is to vary
the placement of the inside points—either close to the center
or out from the center. Alternatively, you can easily use stitches
other than the kiku herringbone, like open squares and hexagons.

Another fascinating option is to fill all the shapes on the ball with
one *hito hude gake* path (see Classic *hito hude gake*, page 126).
Note that when covering the entire ball with a *hito hude gake* path,
only some markings will create a path that goes all the way from
the north pole to the south pole. On the others, you can fill in the
extra stitches individually.

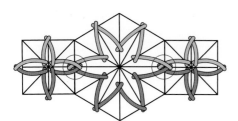

Use kiko herringbone on *hito hude gake* path to fill
squares and hexagons

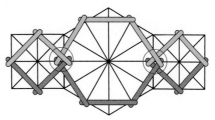

Use other stitches on *hito hude gake* path to fill
squares and hexagons

Classic **Hito Hude Gake** *Design*

Success in completing this design often marks a happy milestone for temari stitchers. Being able to stitch the path correctly requires the ability to see the temari as a whole while also being able to see how the individual parts connect. Before trying this design, become familiar with stitching on a C10 and creating a layered kiku herringbone design (page 91).

This classic design has a kiku herringbone motif stitched with one color thread in the north pole pentagon and a different color in the south pole pentagon. In between, you set up a *hito hude gake* path to fill in the remaining pentagons. After you've tried it on a C10, transfer the technique to a ball marked with 32 or more centers for a very intricate design.

By the time you have the skills to mark and stitch this temari, you should also be able to use your eye to space the stitches rather than measuring with a tape measure. It's quicker and much more satisfying! Before long, you will instinctively be able to judge distances and it will be immediately apparent to you if spacing is off. For more information on measuring by eye, see page 3.

CLASSIC *HITO HUDE GAKE* PATTERN

30 cm (11 ¾") ball wrapped in blue

Sample photographed opposite and on page 24: Maxi-Lock Royal Blue; Kreinik #8 Fine Braid 012HL (metallic purple) and Kreinik #16 Medium Braid 012 (metallic purple) and 091 (metallic yellow); Anchor #5 perle cotton: 298 (yellow) and 87 (pink)

1 Begin by marking a C10 with fine metallic purple (see page 36).

2 Number your path: pin small, numbered slips of paper in the centers of the 12 pentagons to establish the path. Start numbering at the north pole pentagon and spiral around the ball to end at the opposite pentagon, the south pole.

3 Stitch from north pole to south pole with yellow thread. Begin by stitching a herringbone around the north pole. Come up for an outside point just outside the north pole pentagon (red pin in the diagram). Begin stitches for the inside points very close to the pentagon center on the long lines. All stitches for the outside points begin just outside the north pole pentagon on the short lines. Stitch all the way around the north pole and make a jump stitch from the north pole pentagon to pentagon #2. Continue with yellow thread and stitch a *hito hude gake* path through the numbered pentagons, jumping from one to the next across their shared guideline. Note that you will stitch fewer and fewer points in each pentagon as you travel toward the south pole. Stop when you make the first part of the jump stitch into the south pole pentagon (red pin near the south pole in diagram). End off.

4 Stitch a herringbone with pink around the south pole by starting at the outer point (green pin in the diagram). Stitches for the inside points are placed as before, on the long lines near the south pole. Stitches for the outside points are placed just outside the south pole pentagon on the short lines, overlapping the yellow outside points. Spread the two stitches that make up the yellow outside point and stitch around the guideline without catching any of the yellow thread. When you finish the herringbone around the south pole pentagon, make a jump stitch into pentagon #11 and stitch back to the north pole with pink thread, completing the herringbone motif in each pentagon along the way and overlapping the yellow colored outside points. End off.

5 Stitch four more rows using the same two colors (kiku herringbone stitching). Always use yellow to stitch from north to south and pink to stitch from south to north. Continue to layer the outside points.

6 For the last row of each color, add one row metallic yellow to the yellow path and one row medium braid metallic purple to the pink path.

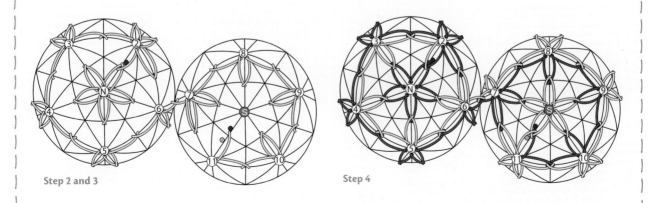

Step 2 and 3   Step 4

Continuous Paths Stitching *(Renzoku Kagari)*

Each of the temari stitching techniques described so far creates a complete motif by stitching along a path that ends up back at the starting point. Tri-wing and herringbone designs, as well as polygons like squares and diamonds, are some of the motifs that are completed with one stitching path. In the last section, we learned how to use the *hito hude gake* technique (one stroke of the brush) to complete motifs in multiple shapes with one stitching path. *Renzoku kagari* (continuous paths stitching) is a slightly different technique that is not really that difficult once you are familiar with the shapes on a combination division. It's made by combining several distinct paths into one design. Each individual

DIAMOND DANCE PATTERN

29 cm (11½") ball wrapped in variegated blue

Sample photographed opposite (front): Maxi-Lock Swirls Blue Winter Ice (variegated blues); Vineyard Silk C-136 (off-white)

1 Begin by marking a C10 with off-white silk thread.

2 Measure the side of a four-part diamond and divide into fifths. With off-white silk thread, stitch four continuous paths through the diamonds (see page 131). Each path should cross the center of the diamond.

3 Using the same method as in Step 2, stitch similar paths in all the diamonds so that each one has threads crossing in both directions. Stitch around all threads crossing the diamond centers to tack them together.

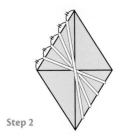

Step 2

Step 3

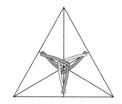

Tri-wings stitched in a triangle

Tri-wings stitched as continuous paths

continuous path ends up back at its starting point and several paths are grouped together to make the design. Each path might travel all the way around the ball or travel around only a portion of the ball before getting back to the starting point. When you are done stitching all the paths, you find that you've created a complete design—the ultimate temari puzzle!

Continuous Tri-wings

Stitching tri-wings in the six-part triangles of a combination division makes a wonderful frame to enclose a floral or geometric motifs stitched in the eight-part squares of a C8 or the ten-part pentagons of a C10. Try stitching a tri-wing on the short lines of the triangle. You can also stitch tri-wings with a series of continuous paths. Instead of making the stitch for the tri-wing's outside point on the short line of the triangle, lay the thread across to the adjacent triangle, without making that stitch at the outside point. Stitch only inside points, laying the thread from triangle to triangle around the ball until you return to your starting point. Continue adding paths until each triangle has a complete tri-wing. To add more rows to the tri-wings, create a pivot point at the centers of the four-part diamonds. You can use keeper pins and, when finished, stitch around all threads at the pivot point if desired.

Look on the opposite page at Refine Your Skills, Variations on Continuous Paths. As you will see, there are endless ways to experiment with continuous paths designs.

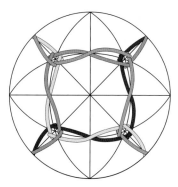

Continuous tri-wings on a C8

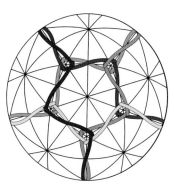

Continuous tri-wings on a C10

Refine Your Skills Variations on Continuous Paths

Try out the same technique on a C6, C8, and C10. The example that follows and the Diamond Dance Pattern (see page 129) both use a diamond shape and you can easily adapt it for different divisions. You'll find some intriguing variations in the final temari design.

To locate your first path for stitching, focus on a diamond shape. Stitch on one side of the diamond (shaded medium blue in the diagram), lay the thread across the diamond center and stitch on the opposite side of that diamond. Shift your orientation so you are looking at the adjacent diamond that is the next one along the path (shaded light blue in the diagram).

The first time you try this technique, place pins along the path to make it easier to follow while stitching. Continue all the way around the ball, stitching on the sides of adjacent diamonds, until you return to your starting point. Now you have completed one path and it's time to add more paths to finish the design. Use the same method of stitching through the diamond shapes, this time placing your stitches closer to the point of each diamond. When you lay the thread across the diamond center, you will create an "X." Complete the remaining paths so each diamond has two threads crossing through it. Add one more set of paths so you have three threads crossing through the center of each diamond and you have a lovely, balanced design.

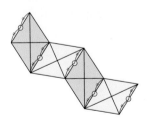

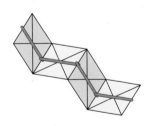

Challenge Designs

The intermediate to advanced patterns here will challenge

you to use a variety of stitches in your repertoire on intricately

marked temari. Each is a test of your skills in executing good

stitching techniques learned on more basic temari patterns.

The fun is solving the puzzle of stitch placement on the

guidelines so the individual motifs combine to create the

entire design. Follow the step-by-step directions to create your

temari works of art.

Rose Design *(Bara)*

This geometric design representing a much loved flower is made
by alternating stitching between two shapes, adding multiple rows
at a time to each. A well-known pattern uses two squares stitched
around an eight-way intersection of guidelines. The techniques
for starting and ending each part of a rose will help you stitch the
design on any division.

1   Square #1: stitch a solid square in the center. Make it large enough
so some of the center is still visible when the second square is added
(usually five or six rows). End off.

2   Square #2: stitch an off-set square on the guidelines not used for the
first square. To begin, bring your thread up next to the last row of the
first square. Lay the thread across the corner of the first square and stitch
next to the first square. To end off, continue stitching until the last row
on the second square just covers the corner of the first square.

Opposite: Raulston Roses, see page 134

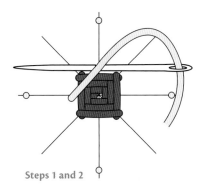

Steps 1 and 2

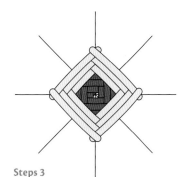

Steps 3

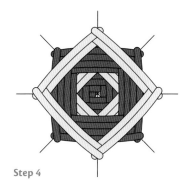

Step 4

3 Ending square #2: continue stitching until the last row on the second square just covers the corners of the first square.

4 Repeat these two steps, alternating between the two squares. The rose is complete when you have filled the design space and the rose is balanced symmetrically.

RAULSTON ROSES PATTERN
31 cm (13 ⅜") ball wrapped in off-white

Sample photographed on page 132: Maxi–Lock Eggshell (off-white); Rainbow Gallery Nordic Gold ND2 (metallic gold); DMC #5 perle cotton: 600 (dark pink), 603 (medium pink), 605 (light pink), 745 (yellow), and 905 (green)

Techniques used: open shapes, page 79; layering, page 92; kiku herringbone, page 99; pine needle stitching, page 63

1 Begin by marking a C8 with fine metallic gold (see page 33).

2 In each eight-part square on the temari, stitch a rose made of two squares. Stitch Square 1 on the long lines (yellow dots in the diagram) and Square 2 on the short lines (white dots in the diagram).

Square #1: five rows yellow, beginning close to the center

Square #1: one row metallic gold, eight rows medium pink

Square #1: one row metallic gold, five rows dark pink, one row metallic gold.

Square #2: one row metallic gold, six rows light pink

Square #2: one row metallic gold, ten rows dark pink

Square #2: one row gold metallic.

3 Stitch a three-petal kiku herringbone design (page 99) around the center of each six-part triangle on the ball. The inside points begin 0.5 cm (3/16") out from center of the triangle on long lines. The outside points begin in the middle of the short lines of the triangle. Stitch three rows light pink and one row dark pink.

4 With green pearl cotton, stitch a hexagon (one row) close to the center of each six-part triangle.

5 With green pearl cotton, stitch pine needle designs to fill the empty spaces. The threads cross in the center of the four-part diamond. With dark pink, stitch around the center of the pine needle design (two stitches) to tack them together.

Mitsubishi and Other Diamond Designs

A layered design takes on new intrigue when stitched on a combination division. One surprising result is a secondary design of diamonds with their points radiating from the center. There are many different ways to create this layered-diamonds design depending on which division you choose and which shapes you decide to stitch. The three examples shown here are just a few of your choices.

As with all layered designs, it's very important keep track of the order of stitching on the shapes within each step of the process. One way is to pin numbered slips of paper to the center of each shape then always follow those numbers when adding rows. Adding more than one row at a time is always an option so long as you are consistent by doing the same for each shape. Review the tips for stitching layered designs on page 92.

With each new row you stitch, take time to true up the shapes (squares, hexagons, pentagons, or other geometric shapes), the emerging diamonds, and the negative space. Watch that your guidelines stay in place. This will result in a temari with a crisp, symmetrical design.

Refine Your Skills Stained Glass Effect and Other Variations

After stitching the first shape, begin each new shape with one row of a contrasting color (green in this diagram) and then finish with the petal color.

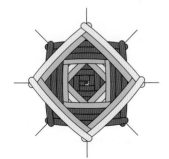

Stained glass effect

Triangles on S6 division

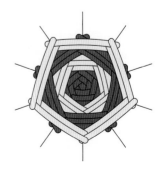

Pentagons on S10 division

All three are made with the same threads: Mitsubishi (front), Yotsubishi (back), Itutsubishi (center)

Three Diamonds (*Mitsubishi*) Pattern

26 cm (10 ¼") ball wrapped in black

Sample photographed opposite (front): Rainbow Gallery Treasure Braid Petite PB14 (metallic gold); DMC #5 perle cotton: 310 (black), 433 (dark brown), 434 (medium brown), 783 (light brown), 725 (dark yellow), and 744 (medium yellow)

Techniques used: open shapes, page 79; layering, page 92

1 Begin by marking a C8 with gold (see page 33).

2 Place a numbered slip of paper in the center of each of the eight-part squares on the ball—there are six of them. Begin with #1 and stitch an open square (one row) on the short lines, just outside the eight-part square.

3 Stitch an open square (one row) around #2.

4 Continue by stitching open squares (one row) around each of the numbers.

5 Begin again at #1 and add one row.

6 Add one row to each of the remaining squares (in number order). Keep adding rows until they meet in the centers of the six-part triangles.

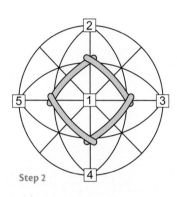

Step 2

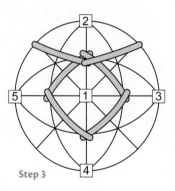

Step 3

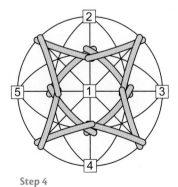

Step 4

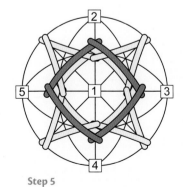

Step 5

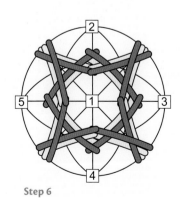

Step 6

Four Diamonds (*Yotsubishi*) Pattern

28 cm (11") ball wrapped in brown

Sample photographed on page 134 (back): Rainbow Gallery Treasure Braid Petite PB14 (metallic gold); DMC #5 perle cotton: 310 (black), 433 (dark brown), 434 (medium brown), 783 (light brown), 725 (dark yellow), and 744 (medium yellow)

Techniques used: open shapes, page 79; layering, page 92

1 Begin by marking a C8 with gold (see page 33).

2 Place a numbered slip of paper in the center of each six-part triangle on the ball—there are eight of them. Stitch a hexagon: place your stitches on the short lines, just outside the six-part triangle (red dots in the diagram). Place your stitches on the long lines inside the triangle and always the same distance from the triangle point (blue dots in the diagram). To figure this distance, you will need to decide how many rows you want to stitch and leave enough room for them to fit in that space.

3 Stitch a hexagon around each six-part triangle.

4 Continue adding rows in layers until you fill the space between the blue dots and the points of the six-part triangles.

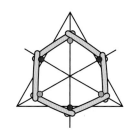

6-part triangle

Step 2

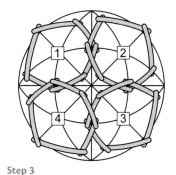

Step 3

Five Diamonds (*Itsutsubishi*) Pattern

31 cm (13 ⅜") ball wrapped in red-brown

Sample photographed on page 134 (center): Rainbow Gallery Treasure Braid Petite PB14 (metallic gold); DMC #5 perle cotton: 310 (black), 433 (dark brown), 434 (medium brown), 783 (light brown), 725 (dark yellow), and 744 (medium yellow)

Techniques used: open shapes, page 79; layering, page 92

1 Begin by marking a C10 with gold.

2 Use the same process that you used for Four Diamonds. Place a numbered slip of paper in the center of each six-part triangle on the ball—there are twenty of them. Follow Step 2 to 4 of Four Diamonds above.

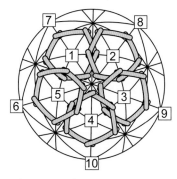

Five Diamonds

Want to put a box weave into
a triangle? Stitch a vertical line
from the point of the triangle
to the middle of the bottom
line of the triangle. Divide that
line into equal parts. Stitch the
remaining vertical lines by laying
them parallel to the first one.
Add horizontal lines with the
same spacing and laying them
parallel to the bottom line of
the triangle.

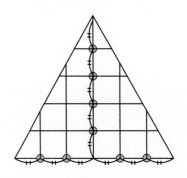

Weaving Techniques to Fill Shapes *(Ami)*

There are many designs that give the illusion of a traditional woven
structure on a temari. The three presented here inspired by techniques
for making baskets, bamboo fences, and caned chair seats. The Japanese
word *kagome* means basket. It translates literally as eyes or holes (*me*) in
the basket (*kago*). The most common type of weaving, hexagonal weaving
(*mutsume*), has a six-sided hole and temari stitchers usually just call this
one *kagome* or basketweave. Other patterns are box weaving (*yotsume*)
which has a four-sided hole and octagonal weaving (*yatsume*) which has
an eight-sided hole.

Begin by adding guidelines on the temari with inconspicuous thread
(sewing thread that is a shade lighter or darker than your thread wrap).
Make sure the guidelines are wrapped snugly and attached securely to the
ball so they don't shift as you work on the design. Decide on the spacing
of your weaving design and place pins along the sides of the shape. This
spacing can vary depending on the size of your shape, thickness of thread,
number of rows, and ultimate intricacy of the design. You can test the
spacing by winding perle cotton around the pins to check the appearance
of the finished design then adjust the pins as you like. Fill the shape by
stitching just inside the marking lines so they are not pulled out of place
while you work. Notice that the threads which cross through the shape
bend and are spaced further apart in the center of the shape than at the
sides. This is because of the curvature of the ball and is more pronounced
in a larger shape. When the woven design is complete, wrap or stitch over
the edges to hide your starts and stops.

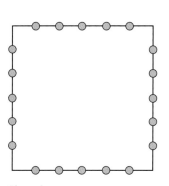
Place pins

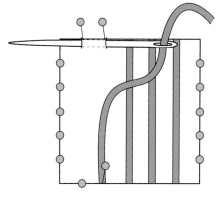
Add vertical lines

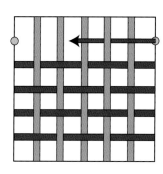
Add horizontal lines

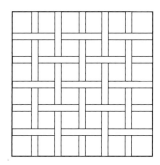
Complete

Box or Square Weaving *(Yotsume Ami)*

This very simple weaving design has threads which cross from two directions. Place pins to divide each side of the shape into equal sections. Next, stitch between the pins to add vertical lines across the square, removing the pins as you go. Place all stitches just inside the guidelines of the square. When stitching between the pins in the horizontal direction, turn your needle around and use the eye end to weave over and under the vertical threads.

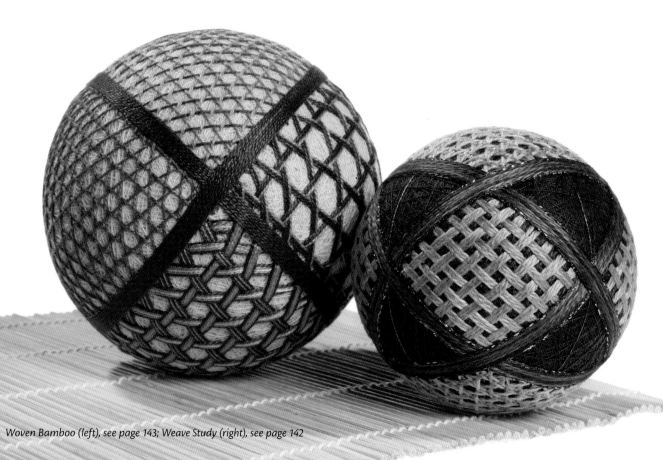
Woven Bamboo (left), see page 143; Weave Study (right), see page 142

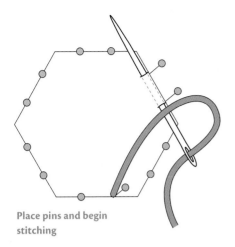

Place pins and begin
stitching

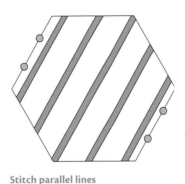

Stitch parallel lines

Add lines in second direction

Hexagonal Weaving to Create a Triaxial Design
(Mutsume Ami)

This relatively easy weaving technique is a classic and among temari
stitchers in Japan. It it is often just called *kagome* (basket). It is composed of
threads crossing from three directions. Use it to fill a triangle or hexagon.
Use the same basketweave technique for maintaining symmetry that you
use for wrapping multiple bands which cross (page 74).

Place pins equally spaced along each side of the shape to be
filled. Stitch to make long lines that run parallel with a side of the
shape, connecting the pins and making sure all stitches are placed just
inside the shape's guidelines. Remove the pins as you go. Repeat the
stitching process for the second direction (shown in red), overlapping
all lines on top of those from the first direction. On the sides without
pins, stitch down into the ball at the end of the stitch from the previous
step. Next, add the lines in the third direction to complete the design
(shown in blue). With each new line, weave to go under the threads
from the first direction (brown in the diagram). Lay it over the threads
from the second direction (red in the diagram). Adding this last woven
set of lines will help threads in all three directions align so regular
hexagons form in the center.

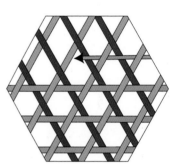

Add lines in third direction

Octagonal Weaving *(Yatsume Ami)*

In chair caning, this weaving technique is called a "double-setting"
design.

Place pins equally spaced along each side of a square. Stitch vertical
lines across the square, removing the pins as you go. Place all stitches just
inside the guidelines of the square. Add a parallel thread right next to
the first so each vertical line is doubled. Next, add horizontal lines, this
time weaving over and under the vertical lines. As before, add a parallel

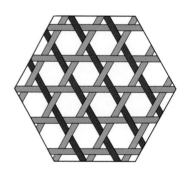

Complete

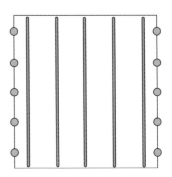

Place pins and stitch vertical lines

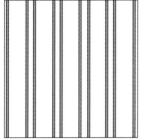

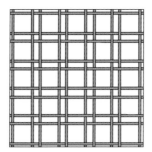

Add horizontal lines

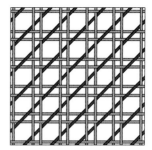

Add diagonal lines

horizontal thread, continuing to weave between stitches. Add diagonal lines which run from lower left to upper right (shown in red). Weave over the horizontal lines and under the vertical lines. Finally, add a diagonal line in the other direction (shown in blue), running from upper left to lower right. Weave over the vertical lines and under the horizontal lines.

WEAVE STUDY PATTERN

28 cm (10 ⁵/₈") ball wrapped in brown

Sample photographed on page 140 (right): Maxi-Lock Cinnamon (brown); Rainbow Gallery Nordic Gold ND 15 (metallic bronze); Caron Watercolors: 123 (variegated tans), 257 (variegated greens), 164 (variegated dark red), 207 (variegated blue greens), and 160 (variegated dark blues)

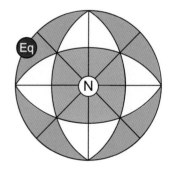

1   Begin by marking a C8 with metallic bronze (see page 33).

2   Fill the eight-part squares around the north and south poles with octagonal weaving. Place nine pins along each side of the square to divide it into ten sections. Stitch the vertical and horizontal lines with tan (remember to stitch two lines for each pin and to weave as you go). Then stitch the diagonal lines in both directions with blue green, weaving through the tan threads as you go.

3   Find the four diamond shapes along the equator (brown in the diagram). Fill each diamond with box weaving. Place seven pins along each side of a diamond to divide it into eight equal sections. With tan thread, stitch between the pins in one direction. Add a row on either side to create a band of three tan threads. Use green thread to stitch a band of three threads in the other direction, weaving over and under the tan thread as you go. Add a background behind the weaving by stitching one row of dark red between each of the bands in the design. Slide the dark red thread under all the tan and green threads.

4   Cover the edges of the woven shapes with wrapped bands: six rows dark blue bordered by one row metallic bronze. See Maintaining Symmetry with Wrapped Bands on page 74 for tips on weaving these bands.

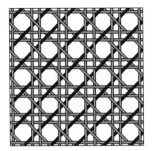

Add diagonal line in other direction

Woven Bamboo Pattern

36 cm (14 $^1/_8$") ball wrapped in off-white

Sample photographed on page 140 (left): Maxi–Lock Eggshell (off-white); Finca #5 perle cotton: 1667 (red), 4228 (green), 8060 (very light brown), 8069 (light brown), 8072 (medium brown), and 8080 (dark brown)

1 Begin by marking an S4 with scrap sewing thread in brown or tan (see page 32). Four slightly different hexagonal weaving designs fill the triangles on the ball.

2 Triangle 1: place guide pins 1 cm ($^3/_8$") apart on the sides of a triangle. With dark brown, stitch lines to connect the pins in the first direction. Add a line in between each of these so they are now spaced 0.5 cm ($^3/_{16}$") apart. You should be able to do this by eye. Repeat in the second direction using light brown thread. Then with green, stitch the lines for the last direction, weaving under the dark brown threads (the first direction).

3 Triangle 2: repeat the steps for Triangle 1 using medium brown thread for all three directions.

4 Triangle 3: place guide pins 1 cm ($^3/_8$") apart on the sides of a triangle. The lines in each direction are three threads wide: light brown, red, and dark brown. Stitch the middle color (red) first between each of the pins for the first direction then add a row of brown on one side and a row of dark brown on the other side of the red. Stitch the remaining two directions in the same manner, weaving the last set under the first.

5 Triangle 4: place guide pins 1 cm ($^3/_8$") apart on the sides of a triangle. The lines in each direction are five threads wide. First stitch the middle color between the pins and then add the remaining colors. Each direction has a different color scheme:

First: dark brown, light brown, red, light brown, dark brown

Second: dark brown, light brown, green, light brown, dark brown

Third: dark brown, light brown, very light brown, light brown, dark brown.

6 Cover the edges of the woven designs by wrapping bands of dark brown, eight rows wide, centered over the scrap thread guidelines.

Flax designs

Stitch a pine needle, then add a herringbone

Flax Leaf *(Asanoha Kagari)*

This geometrical design representing the flax or hemp leaf is one of many traditional Japanese motifs. In temari, the design takes on a different appearance depending on the division and the shape that it fills. Three different methods for creating a flax leaf temari lead to beautiful results:

- **Individual motif:** stitch one flax leaf design to fill a shape

- **Flax leaf all around:** begin with a combination division temari to create a design to cover the entire ball

- **Flax leaf fill:** combine multiples of the design to fill a shape

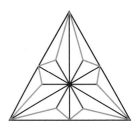

Triangle

Flax Leaf Individual Motif

Creating a single flax leaf is as simple as stitching a pine needle design in the center of your selected shape and then stitching a herringbone as a connecting line around the sides. Vary the shape of the flax leaf by making the pine needle stitches shorter or longer.

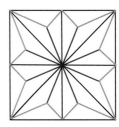

Square

Refine Your Skills Flax Leaf Variations

The photograph opposite shows Flax Leaf created on a C8 division (ball on ground) and on a C10 division (top left). The techniques used for both are pine needle stitching (page 67) and continuous paths stitching (page 129)

The C8 ball is wrapped in blue and marked with metallic white—30 cm (11 ¾ ball). The sample photographed uses Maxi-Lock Blue; Kreinik Medium #16 Medium Braid 032 (white); DMC #5 perle cotton blanc (white). Stitch a flax leaf design all around

the temari with perle white cotton. Tack the centers with white #5 perle cotton.

The C10 ball is wrapped in dark blue and marked with metallic red—37 cm (14½") ball. The sample photographed uses Maxi-Lock Navy (dark blue); YLI Candlelight Metallic Yarn 003 (metallic red); DMC #5 perle cotton 827 (light blue). With light blue perle cotton, stitch a flax leaf design all around the temari. Tack the centers with metallic red.

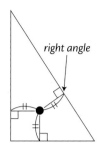

Place pin

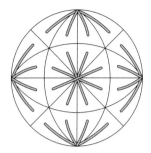

Stitch between pins

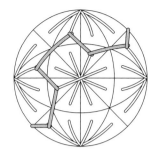

Stitch continuous paths

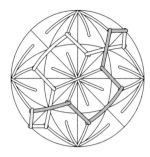

Stitch more continuous paths

Complete

In the diagrams for the triangle and square, the red lines are the pine needle stitches and the blue lines are the herringbone stitches. Tacking the threads crossing through the center of the shape is an option.

Flax Leaf All Around

Pine needle and continuous paths stitching on a combination division create this simple yet stunning, symmetrical design. First, mark the division, then stitch a pine needle design (see page 67) centered in each of the larger shapes (a square for a C8 and a pentagon for a C10). To position the pine needle stitches, place a pin in the center of each small triangle. Check the pin placement by measuring from the pin to the sides of the triangle. Note the right angles. With a little practice, you should be able

COUNTRY NIGHT PATTERN
29 cm (11 $^3/_8$") ball wrapped in tan

Sample photographed on page 144 (top, center): Maxi-Lock Mother Goose (tan); DMC #5 perle cotton blanc (white), 800 (light blue), 815 (red), and 824 (dark blue)

Techniques used: wrapped bands, page 67; cross stitch, page 58; herringbone, page 95; pine needle stitching, page 63

1 Begin by marking a C8 with light blue perle cotton (see page 33).

2 Outline the six-part triangles on the ball with wrapped bands, three rows dark blue on each side of the guideline. With red, stitch a small cross stitch over the bands where they intersect.

3 Stitch a single flax leaf motif in each triangle, half of the eight motifs with white and half with dark blue. Place the pine needle stitches 1.2 cm (½") from the triangle center and then stitch the connecting paths to complete the star shapes.

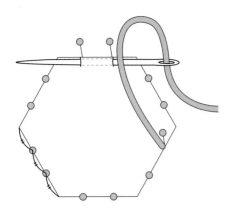

Place pins

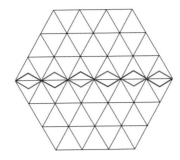

Create a grid and stitch zigzag path

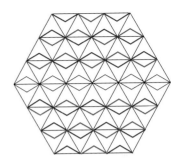

Continue zigzag herringbone stitches
on other guildelines

to place the pin by eye. Stitch between the pins to create the pine needle designs. After completing all the pine needle designs, stitch a continuous path (see page 129) that connects the points of the pine needle designs and passes through the centers of the six-part triangles and through the centers of the four-part diamonds. Tack centers if desired.

Flax Leaf Fill

Fill any shape with multiple flax leaf designs by first stitching a grid to divide the shape into smaller parts. The number of parts in the grid depends on several things: the size of the shape to be filled, the thickness of your stitching thread, and your design preference (intricate with many motifs or simpler with just a few). This is a densely stitched design so take care to make your temari with the outer layer of thread wrapped thick and tight.

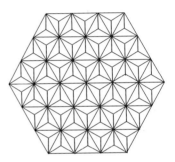

Connect centers of triangles

First, place pins along each side of your shape to divide it into equal parts. A hexagon is shown here with each side divided into three parts. Stitch between the pins to create a grid. Place stitches inside the shape's lines and remove the pins as you go. Adjust the small triangles and the intersections in the center so they are even. Begin filling the grid by stitching a zigzag path, a herringbone with sharp points, along one of the grid lines (red line in the diagram). Place each stitch near the center of the small triangle. You should be able to spot the center of the triangle by eye without measuring. Then lay the thread across the six-way intersection and stitch near the center of the next triangle. Turn the ball and stitch back to your starting point (blue line). Fill the rest of your shape with herringbone stitching across the remaining gridlines. To complete the design, stitch vertical straight stitches which connect the centers of the small triangles. Tacking the centers within the flax leaf design is an optional last step.

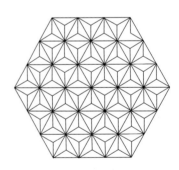

Complete

Filling a square with a flax leaf design is a slightly different process. After creating the grid, stitch the herringbone paths. Turn the ball and stitch the remaining herringbone paths. Finish with straight stitches to connect the triangle centers (see next page).

Filigree Flax Pattern

29 cm (11 3/8") ball wrapped in blue

Sample photographed on page 144 (topmost): Maxi-Lock Chicory (blue); Kreinik Braids #4 Very Fine Braid 032 (metallic white), #8 Fine Braid 032 (metallic white), and #16 Medium Braid 032 (metallic white); DMC #8 perle cotton blanc (white); DMC #5 perle cotton blanc (white), and 824 (blue)

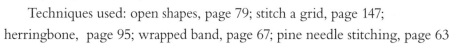

Techniques used: open shapes, page 79; stitch a grid, page 147; herringbone, page 95; wrapped band, page 67; pine needle stitching, page 63

1 Begin by marking an S6 with #8 (fine) metallic white (see page 32).

2 With #8 white perle cotton, stitch an open hexagon around the north pole with the points halfway between pole and equator. Divide each side of the hexagon by three and stitch the grid. Fill with a flax leaf design. Tack the centers with #4 (very fine) metallic white thread. Add rows to the open hexagon to frame your design and cover the starts and stops: two rows white #5 perle cotton, five rows blue, and one row #16 medium metallic white thread.

3 Stitch the same design on the south pole.

4 Obi: on each side of the equator, wrap one row #16 medium metallic white thread, three rows blue perle cotton, three rows white perle cotton, and one row #16 medium metallic white thread. With #8 (fine) metallic white thread, stitch a double herringbone over the equator.

5 Use #8 (fine) metallic white thread to stitch a pine needle design on top of the obi to fill each section between the vertical guidelines.

Flax Fill in Other Shapes

There are endless variations you can try. For instance, fill a triangle or a diamond with a flax leaf design. To fill a square, you will need to stitch herringbone paths in one direction, turn the ball and stitch in the other direction. Then add vertical lines.

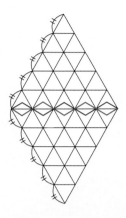

Stitch a grid
Stitch herringbone

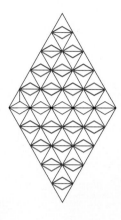

Stitch more herringbone

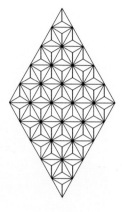

Add vertical lines

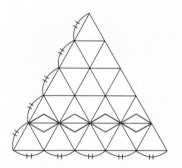

Stitch a grid
Stitch herringbone

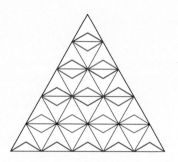

Stitch more herringbone

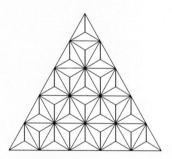

Add vertical lines

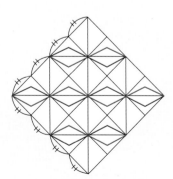

Stitch a grid
Stitch herringbone

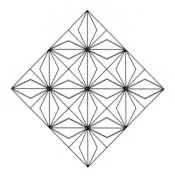

Turn ball and add more herringbone

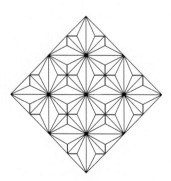

Add vertical lines

More Challenge Patterns

The patterns that follow will really test your skills. If you run into problems, check back with earlier sections of the book so that you completely understand what you are doing. Have fun!

INTERLOCKED PUZZLE PATTERN

32 cm (12 ³/₈") ball wrapped in brown

Sample photographed opposite (right): Maxi-Lock Cinnamon (brown); Rainbow Gallery Nordic Gold ND2 (metallic gold); Anchor #5 perle cotton 307 (orange), 256 (green), 292 (light yellow), and 403 (black).

Techniques used: open shapes, page 79; interlocking, page 89

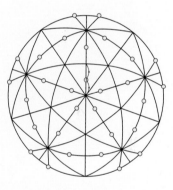

1 Solve the puzzle of stitching interlocked pentagons and diamonds on C10 division while making a colorful temari. Begin by marking a C10 with gold metallic thread (see page 36).

2 Place guide pins at the halfway point on the short lines of each ten-part pentagon.

3 Stitch a small open pentagon around the pins: three rows orange and one row black. Note the diagram shows just one row for clarity. Stitch the same open pentagon in each ten-part pentagon on the ball.

4 Stitch a larger open pentagon with the first row of stitches placed on the short lines of the ten-part pentagon, just outside the pentagon side: three rows green and one row black. Notice how you are stitching around the center of the four-part diamond (on the long lines of the diamond). Stitch the same open pentagon around each ten-part pentagon on the ball and interlock the points.

5 Stitch open diamonds interlocked with the pentagons stitched in Steps 3 and 4. Two diamond points are placed just inside the small orange pentagons stitched in Step 3. The other two diamond points are placed just outside the larger green pentagons stitched in Step 4. Each open diamond is made with three rows light yellow and one row black.

Emerald Isle Pattern

35 cm (13 ¾") ball wrapped in dark turquoise

Sample photographed opposite: Maxi-Lock Dark Turquoise; Rainbow Gallery Treasure Braid Petite PB004 (metallic silver); DMC #5 perle cotton: 796 (dark blue); Vineyard Silk: C-206 (bright blue), C-077 (green), C-037 (medium brown), and T-808 (light brown)

Techniques used: C10 division (page 36); solid hexagon (page 84); french knot (page 60); continuous tri-wings (page 130); layered kiku herringbone designs (page 91)

Several different temari techniques can be combined on the same ball to make a rich and intricate design. The unique placement of two layered kiku herringbone designs creates an interesting negative space in the center of each pentagon. An elegant symmetry is created by the repetition of kiku herringbone designs, hexagons with French knots, and continuous tri-wings around the ball. Richly colored silk threads make this temari glow!

1 Begin by marking a C10 with metallic silver (see page 36).

2 Stitch solid hexagons around the center of each six-part triangle (four rows dark blue perle cotton). With bright blue silk, stitch a French knot in the center of each solid hexagon.

3 Continuous tri-wings: stitch two rows with green silk. Stitches at the inside points are placed next to the solid hexagons from Step 2. Do not stitch at the outside points; carry the thread to the next tri-wing (see page 130 for continuous tri-wing stitching). Tack the threads crossing the diamond centers with dark blue perle cotton. (See page 130 for continuous tri-wing stitching.)

4 Stitch two layered kiku herringbone designs in each ten-part pentagon. Layer by stitching one row at a time on each. On each design, stitch two rows medium brown silk and one row light brown silk. For the first kiku herringbone design, place first row for the inside points near the center of the ten-part pentagon. Place the first row for the outside points 0.5 cm from the tri-wing stitching. For the second kiku herringbone design, place the first row for the inside points 1 cm from the center of the ten-part pentagon. Place the first row for the outside points 0.5 cm from the tri-wing stitching.

5 Fill the center of each kiku herringbone design by stitching around the guidelines: one row bright blue silk and one row dark blue perle cotton.

*Asters. Layered kiku herringbone designs
stitched on 92 faces*

Asters Pattern

44 cm (17 ¼") ball wrapped in light mauve

Sample photographed: Maxi-Lock Boysenberry (light mauve);
Rainbow Gallery Treasure Braid Petite PB201 (metallic yellow);
DMC #8 perle cotton: 819 (light pink), 818 (pink), 554 (violet),
3685 (dark mauve)

Techniques used: C10 division (see page 36); support lines for
multi-centers (page 53); layered kiku herringbone designs (page 91); *hito
hude gake* stitching through multiple shapes (page 124)

A bouquet of autumn asters looks beautiful when stitched on any multi-centers temari.
The sample photographed has 92 centers and you should experiment with other markings. The
pattern here uses a *hito hude gake* (one stroke) path to stitch layered kiku herringbone designs.
Use the same thread colors on the path from north pole to south pole and on the return trip to
the north pole. As an alternative, you could stitch individual flowers in each shape and either
overlap or interlock them (see page 89). This is a good design to stitch on multi-centers temari
that may not be perfectly marked—the intertwined flowers will disguise irregularities in the
pentagon and hexagon shapes.

1 Begin by marking a C10 with metallic yellow. With the same thread, add support lines to make any multi-centers temari. The sample photographed has 92 centers (see page 36).

2 Stitch layered kiku herringbone designs, one in each of the pentagons and hexagons on the ball: one row light pink, one row pink, one row violet, and one row dark mauve. Place the first row for the inside points on the long lines very near the center of each shape. Place the first row for the outside points on the short lines, just outside each shape (pentagon or hexagon). To layer, add one row at a time to each shape. (See page 91 for tips on stitching layered designs.) With most multi-center designs, it is easier to set up a *hito hude gake* (one stroke) path that runs continuously through all the shapes on the ball. Remember that with some markings, there might not be one continuous path that goes through all the shapes. In that case, just fill in the extra shapes after completing each row.

Temari Design and Display

*Colorful and delightful, Japanese temari balls have caught your
eye. You've succeeded in making a nice, round ball and have
learned some of the basic ways to mark it. You've also learned
how to stitch the easier designs. You're hooked! It's not long
before you notice how a simple change in color or placement of
a design on the ball gives it a totally different look. It's time to
begin designing your own temari, the topic of the first part of this
chapter. Whether you have made one or many beautiful temari,
you will need ways to showcase your handiwork. The second part
of this chapter offers ideas for temari display.*

Elements of Temari Design

The notion of designing can be a bit intimidating. How in the world is it
possible to come up with something unique and attractive? The solution
is to practice, play, and experiment! Stitch more temari. Try out lots of
different techniques. Make your temari personal by choosing a favorite
theme. Play around with thread color and texture. Explore filling the
different shapes on temari in a variety of ways. Gaining experience with
stitching variations is the key to jumpstarting your creativity and making
your own temari designs.

   In this section, you will begin by defining goals for each design you
create, deciding exactly what it is that makes each temari special and
basing your design around that. You will also explore color—a powerful
element that can turn a so-so design into a stunning temari. The stitches
you choose and the overall structure you will give your ball are among
the other design decisions you will make along the way.

Opposite; "All-over" designs completely cover the thread wrapped balls

Goal of the Design

First, think about your goal for your new project. Are you making the temari in order to study a certain technique? Then select highly contrasting colors so you can easily see the result of your efforts. The temari's division and the stitches you use will be dictated by the technique. Try the same stitch to fill various shapes in different divisions to discover all the ways the stitch can be used. Also try different arrangements—interlocked or layered designs, for example.

Is your goal to give this temari as a gift or to make a commissioned piece to sell? In either of these cases, the design should be inspired by the recipient. Careful consideration of color and symbolism are especially appreciated. Interview the recipient to discover color preferences and personal qualities so you can select meaningful and appropriate symbolic motifs. For instance, a crane, symbolizing long life, makes an excellent motif for a birthday gift. The bamboo plant, which exhibits strength and flexibility, could be used as part of a design meant for encouragement in one of life's many trials. The temari division is dictated by the amount of time you will spend on the piece. A basic rule is that more stitches equals more time. A simple division temari will be finished much more quickly than a combination division yet can be just as striking with the right choice of colors and motifs.

Is this temari intended as a treat for just for you? Then it's time to explore! Use your favorite colors, flowers, and symbolic motifs. Create this temari as part of a set or to display singly as a small work of art. Follow your whims in choosing between the many possible variations and stitch a temari that makes you feel happy and content, not only while you are stitching but afterwards when you add it to your collection.

Whatever goal you have in mind, experimenting to come up with a new design requires you to be willing to make a test temari or two. When an idea doesn't work or needs a slight change in color or stitching, either pull out the stitches on your first effort or make another temari. Keep trying. You will eventually be rewarded with a design of your own that delights the eye and satisfies the soul.

Color

Temari with basic designs on simple divisions are so quick to make that you can easily experiment with different combinations and shades of color. Often the colors you select are dictated by the purpose: holiday decorations, gifts, favorite colors of the recipient, seasonal colors, and so on. When you're not sure where to begin with color selection, look around your home for inspiration. A bit of fabric from a favorite dress or pillow cover can inspire your choice of colors for temari. If you are interested in color theory, keep a color wheel with your temari tools for checking color combinations and for help in adding a shade. There are many excellent books to help guide you through your color selection. Check out the bibliography in the back of this book for some good books on color.

One of my favorite ways to choose colors is to follow Mother Nature's lead and study a photo taken outdoors. When I find a particularly striking picture—something that really catches my eye—I know the colors in it work well together. A fun way to experiment with color is to upload the photo to an online website with a program to pick the predominant colors. Print the result and take it to a local needlework shop or use a manufacturer's sample chart to match threads. First pull threads to match the strongest colors and then select shades to add to the palette.

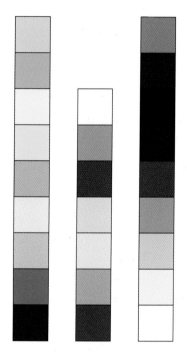

Left: Daffodil palette
Middle: Seashore palette
Right: Woodland palette

Several of the color palettes used to design the temari in this book were inspired by photographs. The colors for the open and solid shapes temari (pages 84 to 85) came from a photograph of brilliantly colored daffodils against a blue sky. A palette created from a photo of the seashore was used to make the merry-go-round temari (page 110 to 114). And nature's colors of the woods inspired the threads selected for mitsubishi and other diamond designs (page 136).

Once you've chosen the basic two or three colors, consider if you will use a number of different shades. Shading can be done within each color (from light to dark) or between colors to connect them and add cohesiveness to your design. Shading adds depth to the design and thread companies are happy to supply you with lots of choices. Another option is to use strongly contrasting colors as accents to make the design "pop." Adding one last row to a motif in a strong yet different color is often the finishing touch that makes the temari really eye-catching.

Symbolism

Symbolism is a very important part of the art of temari as well as other arts and crafts in Japan. Make a very special gift for someone by considering the occasion and the person. Browse the list opposite for inspiration in choosing appropriate designs and colors. When you are finished stitching the temari, make a little card listing the ingredients in the ball and the symbolism of the design. The recipient will love the gift even more and the whole process will be rewarding and meaningful for you. Remember: seasonal patterns always work!

Give Meaning to Your Temari

Bamboo (*take*): resilience and strength, constancy, integrity and honor. Make the stems with wrapped bands and straight stitches (for the joints). Leaves can be made with spindles and fly stitch.

Bellflower (*kikyo*): sign of autumn. On a simple 10 division temari, stitch a five-petal kiku herringbone design in blue.

Bridge (*hashi*): link between this world and the next

Carp (*koi*): perseverance, faithfulness in marriage, and general good fortune. Fish are fun to design with solid diamonds for the body. Add fins with straight stitches and eyes with French knots.

Cherry blossoms (*sakura*): most beloved flower, transience of life due to brief life of the blossoms, a sign of spring. This five-petal flower is often stitched in shades of pink using kiku herringbone stitching. Other cherry designs are created with negative space designs similar to Buttercups on page 168.

Chrysanthemum (*kiku*): endurance, long life, integrity. The kiku's many petals are often created by using kiku herringbone stitching. There are many other ways to represent the flower; for instance, straight stitches radiating from a central point.

Circle (*maru*): perfection, continuity of life, endless circle of the seasons. The shape of the temari itself symbolizes perfection. Create a sampler of the seasons by stitching different flowers in the shapes on the divided ball.

Crane (*tsuru*): longevity, closely associated with New Year, weddings, and births. This popular temari design can be stylized entirely with straight stitches. Or stitch the wings with kiku herringbone and add the other features with straight stitches.

Cricket (*korogi*): bravery and the fighting spirit

Diamond (*hishi*): an amulet that guards the four corners of the home. Solid or open diamond shapes are often overlapped or interlocked.

Dog (*inu*): protection of young children

Dragonfly (*tombo*): martial success, victory. Make the wings of spindles or large, lazy daisy stitches. The body and tail of the dragonfly can also be made with spindle stitching.

Fan (*ogi*): auspicious motif represents increase and a good omen for the unfolding future. Use pine needle stitching in the shape of a fan.

Firefly (*hotaru*): passionate love or martial spirit

Geese (*gacho*): bearers of happiness

Hemp (*asa*): burned at summer's Obon festival to help departed spirits find their way; seen on children's kimono as parents' wishes for them to grow strong and healthy. Many ways to stitch this auspicious design are shown in the section on Flax Leaf stitching.

Hexagon (*kikkou*): tortoise shell, representing long life

Mandarin ducks (*oshidori*): conjugal fidelity and joy

Pine (*matsu*): longevity, good fortune, steadfastness, virtue. Use some of the many variations for pine needle stitching or free embroidery to create an entire tree.

Spider (*kumo*): industry

Waves (*name*): power and resilience. Swirl stitching is perfect for symbolizing waves.

Willow (*yanagi*): flexibility and strength. Use a stem stitch and free embroidery to create the drooping branches of a willow.

Stitches

Much of this book is focused on individual stitches and how to combine them to create individual motifs like squares, tri-wings, and herringbone designs. Glance through the Visual Reference starting on page 181 for a quick reference to your choice of stitches. When planning your temari design, select stitches that suit the theme and will fit into the shapes on your chosen division. Is the theme floral? The herringbone is an excellent choice for stitching flowers of all sorts. A solid diamond could represent a leaf in a floral design or become part of a geometric puzzle when combined with other shapes like squares or triangles. To understand the function of each stitch, ask yourself what can be done with the stitch. Is it suitable for filling squares or hexagons? What kind of pattern does it make when repeated or combined with other stitches? A temari design can be very simple with only one or two types of stitching, or it can be more intricate with several types layered over one another or interlocked together. Let your creativity bloom by experimenting with combining traditional temari stitches with surface embroidery and beading.

Structure

At the same time that you are considering different colors and stitches for your design, think about the shapes within all the different temari divisions and the many possible arrangements of those shapes.

The most basic structure, a simple division, offers two hemispheres that can be filled with matching motifs, one at the north pole and another at the south pole. The number of vertical guidelines dictates the complexity of the design: more guidelines mean a more intricate design. The equator between the hemispheres can be decorated with wrapped or stitched designs.

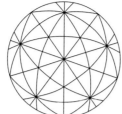

Look for shapes on C8 and C10

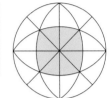

Cube

Even more intricate designs are possible with the more complex structure of combination divisions. Learn to take advantage of the main shapes on the C8 and C10 by isolating and filling each with its own motif. Notice how there are six squares on a C8, just as there are six squares on a cube. Each square on the C8 has an eight-way intersection of threads at its center. This arrangement naturally lends itself to fills like solid squares, open squares, or herringbone designs with four or eight petals.

Another option for the C8 is focusing on the eight triangles (like the eight triangles of an octahedron). Each triangle has a six-way intersection of threads at its center so is particularly suited to being filled with tri-wings or solid or open triangles. The ever versatile herringbone could be used to make flowers with three or six petals.

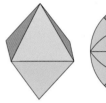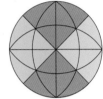

Eight triangles of octahedron

Another arrangement of triangles that is found on the C6 or C8 resembles a tetrahedron and has four large triangles, each with a six-way intersection of threads at the center. The symmetry of this mathematical shape is particularly appealing.

When stitching on a C10, you have options similar to the C8—you can fill the triangle or diamond shapes. You can also design for pentagons, each of which has a ten-way intersection of threads at the center. This division has twelve pentagons nested side by side like the dodecahedron. These shapes can be filled with five-point stars, solid or open pentagons, or herringbone designs with five or ten petals.

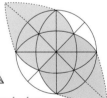

Four triangles of tetrahedron

Finally, play "the string game" to discover other shapes hidden in the temari's guidelines. Explore how you could isolate those shapes and combine them with other shapes on the ball. First mark the ball in a combination division, adding support lines to create a multi-centered marking if you want a more intricate puzzle. Look for shapes like hexagons, rectangles, stars, or kites, and place pins at the corners. Wind

Dodecahedron

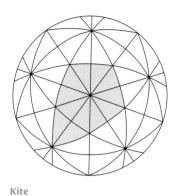

Kite

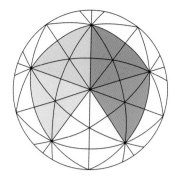

Triangles

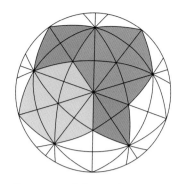

Hexagons and diamonds

string (or perle cotton) around the pins to isolate the shapes. Add more pins to mark other shapes and continue winding the string around them. Play around with the arrangement of shapes until you have a pleasing design that covers the entire ball. Then outline the shapes by stitching between the pins, removing the pins and wrapped string as you go. Fill each of these shapes to make a temari that is your own unique creation.

All-Over Designs

Totally covering the thread-wrapped ball with stitching is one of temari's ultimate challenges! As you can see from the drawings in the section on Structure (page 163), you can stitch solid shapes to cover the entire ball. Begin stitching in the center of each shape and continue until you reach the outside border. On the C8, choose the squares, triangles, or diamonds. On the C10, choose the pentagons, triangles, or diamonds. All-over designs can also be made by using wrapping techniques or by combining wrapping with stitching shapes. Another option is stitching larger shapes that overlap. They can be interlocked or layered. When wraps or shapes are stitched in a layered fashion, you always get a surprise just as you are completing the ball and new shapes appear in different arrangements!

Refine Your Skills Sharing Guidelines

As you continue to explore a temari's structure, take advantage of the way shapes are nested side-by-side around the temari. Extend the motif stitched in a shape across the guideline shared with its neighboring shapes. Play around with interlocking or layering the motifs across the shared guidelines.

Stitching across shared guidelines

Here are a few tips to help you complete the perfect all-over temari:

- Start with a small ball, about 22 cm or 23 cm (8 ⁵/₈" or 9"), and make it as round as possible.

- Create a very firm surface so the dense stitching will hold in place.

- For the thread wrap, choose a neutral color (grey) or one of the colors of your stitching thread.

- Marking thread should be thin and just a shade different from the thread wrap color. Or mark with a thicker, bolder thread and plan to remove it before adding the last few rows of stitching.

- All-over designs use a lot of thread, so be sure to have a full skein of each color on hand.

- Lay the thread in straight lines to keep your stitched shapes even.

- To get better coverage on the ball, let the tension of your stitching be rather loose so the threads rest nicely on the ball and are not stretched.

- Maintain the same distance between your stitches so they are all evenly spaced; watch the negative space as you go to make sure.

- If spacing is a problem for you, mark the halfway point along each line and complete the stitching on all shapes to that point.

- When you are nearing completion, place a 1 cm or 0.5 cm circle guide at each ending point to check that each row you add is the same distance from the ending point. Then remove the circle guides and add the last few rows.

- As you add new rows and especially just before finishing, nudge previous rows together to make sure the ball is adequately covered.

When you've perfected all these skills, the last rows will meet and the ball will be totally covered with stitching. For your first try, practice the techniques by stitching solid shapes in any of the divisions. When you've got it, try out another pattern, like Abstracted Stars (see page 167).

Four Tops (see page 167)

ABSTRACTED STARS PATTERN

25 cm (9 ¾") ball wrapped in grey

Sample photographed on page 156 (left): Maxi-Lock Grey; sewing thread for marking, dark grey; Anchor #5 perle cotton: 386 (light yellow), 293 (medium yellow), 264 (light green), 266 (medium green), 95 (light purple), 98 (medium purple), and 101 (dark purple).

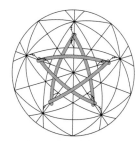

1 Begin by marking a C10 with dark grey (see page 36).

2 Stitch layered five-point stars centered in each of the twelve pentagons on the ball. Select three colors (for example, yellow, green and purple) and choose a light and medium shade of each. Stitch two stars with each of these six thread colors. Place stars of the same color opposite each other on the ball. Since this is a layered design, you will need to keep track of your order of stitching (see page 36 for layering tips). Stitch one row at a time on each star with the stitches for the first row placed halfway along the short lines of the ten-part pentagons. Continue adding rows, in the same order, until the points meet in the pentagon centers.

3 Outline with dark purple. Stitch single straight stitches along the sides of the triangles formed in Step 2.

FOUR TOPS PATTERN

28 cm (11") ball wrapped in dark green. The larger ball (back) is 32 cm (12 ½")

Sample photographed opposite: Maxi-Lock Spruce (dark green); Rainbow Gallery Treasure Braid Petite PB57 (metallic green); Caron Watercolors: 209 (medium purple), 201 (green), 267 (light purple), 144 (orange), and 275 (yellow)

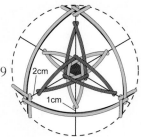

Techniques used: C6 division, four-centers design, open triangle, solid hexagon, interlocked tri-wings (page 117). Four large triangles on a C6 are nested side by side and create a very attractive symmetry. An easy way to locate them is to outline the triangle shapes with thread and then fill the centers.

1 Begin by marking a C6 temari with metallic green (see page 34).

2 Stitch an open triangle around the outside of a large six-part triangle (three rows green, two rows medium purple). Only one row green is shown in the diagram for clarity. Stitch three more similar open triangles, interlocking all triangles at their points.

3 Stitch a solid hexagon (four rows) with medium purple around the six-way intersection of guidelines in the center of each triangle stitched in Step 2. Notice how these hexagons are equidistant.

4 Stitch two interlocked tri-wings around the hexagon from Step 3. For the first one, stitch on the short lines of the six-part triangle (three rows bright green, one row light purple). For the inside points, place the first row next to the purple hexagon. For the outside points, place the first row 1 cm from the edge of the triangle stitching from Step 2. For the second tri-wing, stitch on the long lines of the six-part triangle (three rows orange, one row yellow). Interlock with the first tri-wing by weaving over and under it between stitches. For the inside points, place the first row next to the green tri-wing. For the outside points, place the first row 2 cm from the six-way intersection of guideline threads located at the corner of the large triangle stitched in Step 2.

Negative Space Designs

The areas on a temari that are not covered with stitching are called *negative spaces*. Sometimes, you'll want to fill them with pine needles, flax, weaving, or other interesting fill stitches. However, when the negative space is the focus of your design, the shape of the unstitched, thread-wrapped area grabs your eye first. As with all temari stitching, watch the negative space change with every new row to make sure you are stitching evenly. You can easily compensate when a negative space goes off kilter by making small adjustments with each new row. Leave a bit more space between rows or pack them closer together. A quick and easy negative space design like Buttercups can be made on a simple division temari with herringbone stitching overlapping the equator. This design is similar to a merry-go-round (page 114) except for a slightly different placement of the first row.

BUTTERCUPS PATTERN
26 cm (10 ¼") ball wrapped in bright yellow

Sample photographed opposite: Maxi-Lock Gold (bright yellow); Treasure Braid Petite PB201 (metallic yellow); Anchor #5 perle cotton: 185 (light teal), 187 (medium teal), 189 (dark teal)

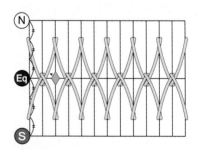

1 Begin by marking an S12 with metallic yellow (see page 32).

2 Stitch layered kiku herringbone designs over the equator. The inside points begin a third of the distance from the pole and the outside points begin just over the equator. Stitch one row in each hemisphere with light teal. For the inside points on the second row, take the stitch 1 cm from the first row. For all remaining rows, place stitches at the inside points around and just below all previous rows as usual. Total number of rows is five rows light teal and three rows medium teal.

3 With dark teal, stitch a solid diamond to fill the negative spaces at the equator.

Symmetry

The symmetry of a temari design draws in our eyes and fascinates our minds. Each ball has at least two kinds of symmetry. *Rotational symmetry* is seen by looking at each motif head–on and noticing how it is evenly arranged around the center intersection of threads. *Translation symmetry* comes from locating identical motifs and noting their placement around the ball. Many temari artists love temari for their symmetry and feel that the most beautiful balls are the most symmetric. So, when you are designing, consider the symmetry you can create. Repetition of stitches and colors is a valuable design tool within each motif and in the arrangement of identical motifs around the temari.

Visual Unity of a Design

As the final step in creating your new temari, look at the finished ball and ask yourself a few questions. Does it look like it's finished? You may need to add a bit more stitching to connect some of the stitched areas. The opposite can happen if the finished temari simply looks too crowded with unrelated stitches and colors. Do you notice something that seems like it just doesn't belong? No one element should stand out as being totally different unless you truly want just one focal point on the ball. Your eye should move easily around the design without being blocked—taking care with the symmetry created in your design can really help with this. Some of your temari creations will definitely stand out above the others. Trust your eyes and study these to figure out why they are so special. You can trust your innate sense of visual unity.

Temari Display

One of the first things that people ask about temari is "What do you do with them?" Temari balls can be used as toys by children like they were hundreds of years ago, but more often they are displayed as art objects in the home. People often think of them as holiday ornaments because of their spherical shape, sparkly metallic threads, and bright colors. However, if that is the only way you display them, you are missing out on colorful home décor for all seasons.

In interior design stores, you can find large bowls filled with orbs made of everything from glass and ceramic to wood and rattan. They are mass-produced and often catch the eye. Why not create these decorations yourself in colors to match your room? Use the same color palette to stitch a bowlful of temari with different designs, all coordinated in color yet each one unique in pattern.

There are many more ways to display your temari creations. For example, a large glass vase or jar filled with temari creates a unique and three-dimensional focal point for a room. Select temari with colors and designs to match the season. Use smaller temari to decorate drawer pulls, doorknobs, scrolls, handbags or necklaces; use larger ones for Christmas trees, mobiles or a special focal piece. Display your beautiful designs in small groups or individually. Take your temari along to the shop to select the perfect display stand for a single temari. Napkin rings and candle stands are often the perfect size and come in a myriad of different shapes and colors.

Another choice for display of a single ball is to make a zabuton, a tiny fabric pillow, to match the temari. Square shaped pillows are easiest to make or you can use the following technique to make any shape you wish. Adjust the size so the pillow is about the same width as the temari.

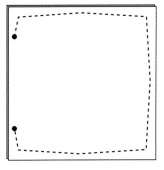

Step 2

Making a Zabuton for Display

1   Cut two 5" (12.5 cm) squares of fabric. Satins or brocades will have a luxurious shine or you can use any woven fabric with a texture and color to complement your temari.

2   Pin the squares right sides together. Draw a ¼" seam allowance around the edge. Redraw the stitching line by bringing each corner point in about ¼" (black dashed line on diagram). This adjustment will result in corners that are nicely square when you are finished.

3   Stitch along the adjusted line drawn in Step 2, leaving an opening for turning and filling. Trim seam allowances at corners.

4   Turn the pillow right side out and fill. For a nicely weighted pillow use rice hulls, small beans or plastic beads for filling.

5   Hand stitch the opening closed with small stitches so the seam is inconspicuous. Adjust the filling evenly if needed.

6   Optional: put a dimple in the center of your pillow by making a tacking stitch through all layers at the center of the pillow. Add tassels or other embellishment.

Hanging Temari Display

A temari dangling from a hanger spins in the air showing off all its beauty. In the past, formal temari in Japan were displayed with very long tassels and elaborate hangers. These were called *gotenmari*. Later the name fell out of common usage so that today they would simply be called temari. Add a simple thread hanger or a fancy tassel and a dragon-knotted cord to your temari for this type of display.

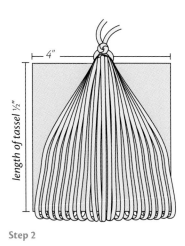

length of tassel 1/2"

4"

Step 2

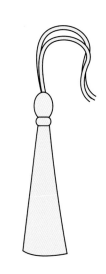

Step 3

Making a Simple Thread Hanger Cut a length of thread for the hanger, about 8" (20 cm) long, and thread one end onto your needle. Take a small stitch deep into the temari thread wrap where you want to attach the hanger. Remove the needle, knot the ends of the thread together, and trim the tail very short. Rotate the knot to the surface of the temari and give it a tug to pull the knot under the surface.

Adding a Tassel To add a touch of elegance, stitch a tassel to the bottom of a temari that you plan to hang. Purchase tassels in the home decor department of fabric stores or make your own from the threads used to stitch the ball.

1   Wrap the threads for the tassel: cut a piece of cardboard 4" (10 cm) wide and slightly longer than the desired length of the tassel. Wind the tassel thread around the cardboard until the tassel is thick enough (about 30 times, depending on the type of thread). Be careful to not stretch the thread when winding.

2   Secure the wraps. Cut an 18" (46 cm) length of thread, pass it under the wraps, and tie a firm overhand knot at the top of the tassel. The ends of this thread will be used later to stitch the tassel to the temari. Slip the tassel off the cardboard and smooth the lengths of thread.

3   Create the neck of the tassel. Cut another 18" (46 cm) length of thread and tie it securely just under the "head" of your tassel with an overhand knot. Keep ends of the 18" length of thread from Step 2 free of the knot. Wrap thread end around tassel several times and tie off. Thread each loose end in a needle and stitch it through the wrapped area to hide the ends.

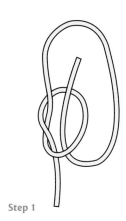

Step 1

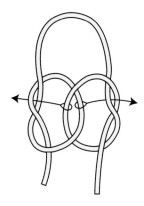

Step 2

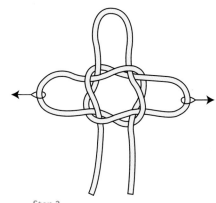

Step 3

4 Finish the tassel. Straighten the threads of the tassel skirt before trimming them to their finished length. If the tassel threads are wrinkled, hold them over steaming water and smooth them straight. To get a nice straight cut across the bottom, first wrap the threads in a wide strip of scrap paper. Then cut through the paper and threads in one cut.

Attaching the Tassel to the Temari The tassel can be stitched to the bottom of the temari ball so the head touches the ball or you can leave a little space, depending on the look you prefer. To attach the tassel to the temari, thread a needle with one of the long threads at the top of the tassel, left for this purpose. Enter the needle in the ball at the point where you want the tassel to hang—often on the equator. Take several zigzag stitches underground. Come up and cut the thread close to the surface of the ball. Then thread the needle with the second free thread, enter the ball near the first thread, and stitch underground in the same manner.

Simple Decorative Good Luck Knot
Dress up your temari hanger by using a decorative cord and tying a good luck knot. Attach it either to the top or the bottom of the temari. The cord should be more than 1mm wide for a nice sized knot. A slightly stiffer cord like rattail (satin cord) will be easier to tie than a soft one.

1 Start with an 18" (46 cm) long cord folded in half with a loose overhand knot, as shown in the first diagram.

2 Tie a second interlocked overhand knot following the thread path on the second diagram.

3 Tighten and adjust the loops. Pull the sides of the knot out as shown with arrows in the Step 2 and Step 3 diagrams. Slowly tighten, adjusting the size of the loops carefully so that they are evenly sized.

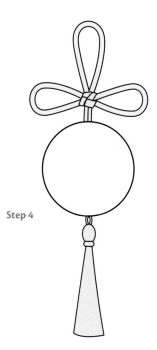

Step 4

4 Attach the hanger to the temari. Attach each end of the cord separately to the temari by pulling it through the thread wrap with a large eye needle. Take a couple of stitches back and forth under the thread wrap until the cord is secure. Since this cord will support the weight of the temari, be careful to check that it will not pull out when hanging. If you used a very thick cord to tie the knot, you will need to stitch it to the ball with sewing thread in a matching color.

Keeping a Temari Journal

Your most important tools in designing temari will be your memory of all the temari you've made and your inspiration for future stitching. Keeping a record of your progress in a journal or on a computer is essential. You can refer to it when you want to repeat a success and when you need ideas for that special gift for family or friends. You'll be able to see your progress and improvement as you explore different stitching techniques and work your way through temari divisions. Even your pattern writing skills will improve as you make notes about each temari. It's handy to keep the journal right in your stitching basket so you can jot down notes as you make the ball, mark it, and stitch the design. If you keep a journal on a computer, make notes on an index card while you stitch so transferring them to the computer later will be quick and easy. Keep your notes concise by referring to the following list of the important things you'll need to know about this temari if you were to stitch it again in the future.

- Start date.
- Origin of pattern; if this is your own design, then jot down your inspiration.
- Threads used (brand and color number).
- Size of ball and type of division.
- Stitching process, recorded step-by-step. Each step should give the starting points for the stitches, the number of rows, color of thread, and technique (interlocked, layered, etc).

- Diagram (colored pencils) and photograph
- Special challenges and how you overcame them.
- Date of completion
- Use—what you did with the ball when finished. Was it a gift or an addition to your collection?

In a separate section of your journal, record ideas that inspire you: swatches of colored paper or fabric, photographs of temari you want to make, poetry or descriptive prose, a list of the symbolism of different motifs (Japanese and Western), photographs that you love for their color or composition, or colorful doodles for possible future designs. This section of your journal will become a scrapbook for your growing creativity in making new temari designs.

Appendices

Bibliography

Arai, Tomokazu. *Furusato no Temari (Hometown Temari)*. Published in Japanese in 1990.

Baird, Merrily. *Symbols of Japan*. New York: Rizzoli International Publications, Inc., 2001.

Beyer, Jinny, *Color Confidence for Quilters*. California: The Quilt Digest Press, 1992.

Hibi, Sadao, *The Colors of Japan*. Tokyo: Kodansha International, 2000.

Mashima, Takashi and Yoriko Noda. *The Gotenmari Photo Collection*. Published in 1997 in Japanese.

Ozaki, Chiyoko. *Kyodo no Temari (Folk Temari, Tradition and Creation)*. Published in Japanese by Macaw, 1990.

Rees, Yvonne. *Caning and Rushwork*. London: Wardlock, 1995.

Rinne, Melissa M. *Masters of Bamboo: Artistic Lineages in the Lloyd Cotsen Japanese Basket Collection*. Asian Art Museum, 2008.

Suess, Barbara B. *Japanese Temari*. Elmhurst (Chicago): Breckling Press, 2007.
Suess, Barbara B. *Japanese Kimekomi*. Elmhurst (Chicago): Breckling Press, 2008.

Wolfrom, Joen. *ColorPlay*. California: C&T Publishing, 2000.

Vintage temari from the collection of Barbara Suess

Sources for Temari Making Supplies

First, check your stash! Recycle leftovers from other crafts. Support your local needlework or fabric shop by shopping there first. You will find all kinds of interesting threads and materials for embellishing temari. If there is no shop in your area, check out the online sources listed here.

Threads

Anchor: available from Coats and Clark at www.coatsandclark.com
The Caron Collection: www.caron-net.com
DMC: www.dmc-usa.com
Finca: www.presenciausa.com
Maxi-Lock serger thread: www.amefird.com/products-brands/ consumer-products
Rainbow Gallery: www.rainbowgallery.com
Sulky: www.sulky.com
Vineyard Silk: www.vineyardsilk.com
YLI: www.ylicorp.com

Circle Guides

Use these circles to space stitches evenly around a center.

Other

My website includes a selection of threads, as well as several specialty supplies designed for temari enthusiasts, such as the v-ruler. Visit www. japanesetemari.com.

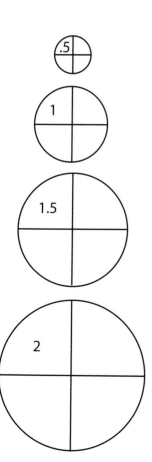

Left Hand Stitching Guide

Come up at 1, go down at 2, up at 3, down at 4, etc.

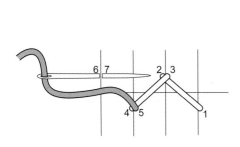

Herringbone

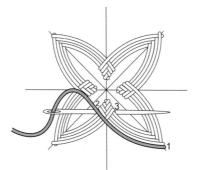

Kiku herringbone

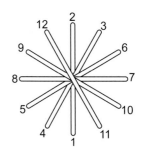

Pine needle

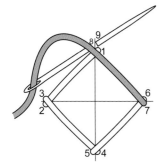

Square

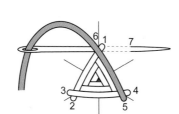

Triangle

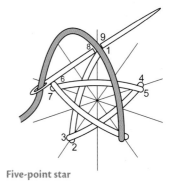

Five-point star

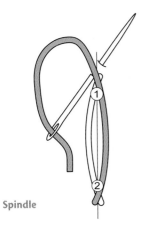

Spindle

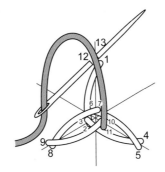

Tri-wing

C10 Number Chart

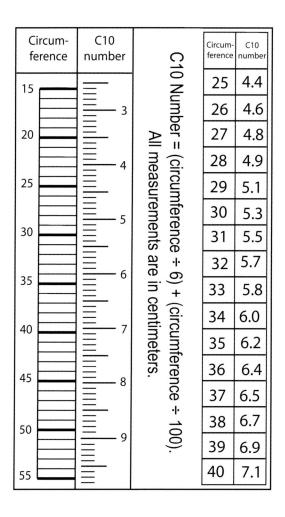

C10 Number = (circumference ÷ 6) + (circumference ÷ 100). All measurements are in centimeters.

Circum-ference	C10 number
15	
	3
20	
	4
25	
	5
30	
35	6
40	7
45	8
50	9
55	

Circum-ference	C10 number
25	4.4
26	4.6
27	4.8
28	4.9
29	5.1
30	5.3
31	5.5
32	5.7
33	5.8
34	6.0
35	6.2
36	6.4
37	6.5
38	6.7
39	6.9
40	7.1

Visual Reference

Simple Division

Where Am I?

If you always keep a white pin at the north pole, it is easy to keep track of where you are.

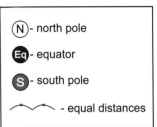

- N - north pole
- Eq - equator
- S - south pole
- ⌢⌢ - equal distances

Diagram notations, page 2

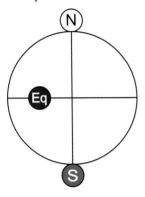

S4 division, page 31

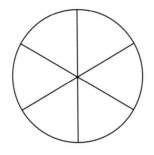

S6 division, page 32

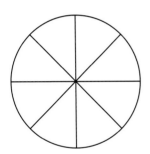

S8 division, page 32

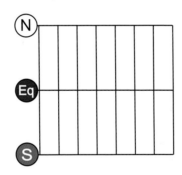

S8 division, flat view, page 32

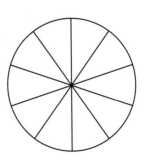

S10 division, page 32

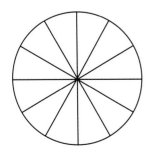

S12 division, page 32

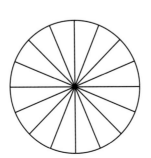

S14 division, page 32

Combination Divisions

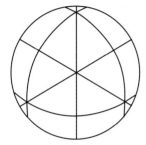

C6 division, page 34

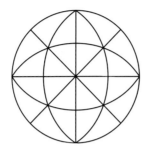

C8 division, page 33

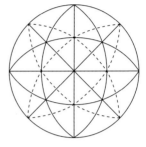

Double eights division, page 32

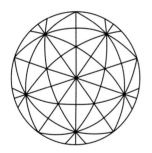

C10 round view, page 36

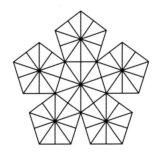

C10 flat view, page 36

Support Guidelines

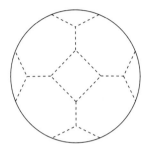

14 faces, without guidelines, page 46

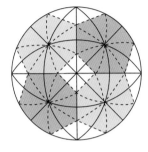

14 faces, with guidelines, page 46

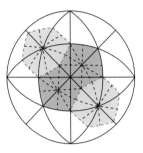

16 faces design, page 50

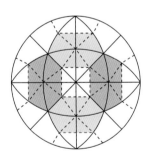

18 faces design, page 51

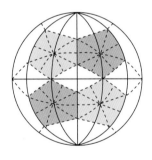

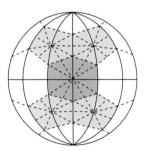

20 faces design, page 48

Multi-Centers

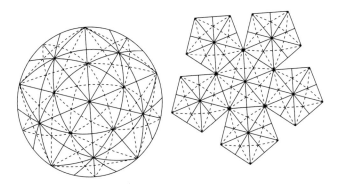
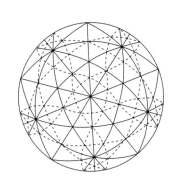

32 centers marking, page 53

42 centers marking, page 53

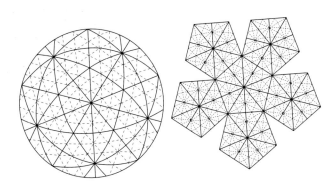
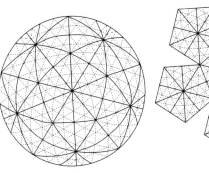
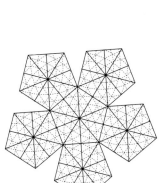

92 centers marking, page 55

122 centers marking, page 54

Surface Embroidery Stitches

Chain stitch, page 58

Detached chain stitch,
page 59

Couching, page 59

Cross stitch, page 58

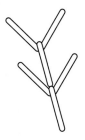

Fly stitch, page 60

French knot, page 60

Stem stitch, page 59

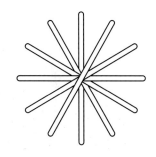

Pine needle stitch, page 63

Partial pine needles, page 65

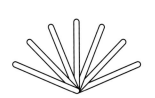

Fan, page 63

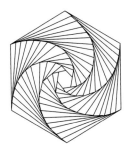

Swirl stitching, page 65

Wrapping

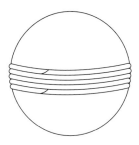

Basic wrapped bands, page 69

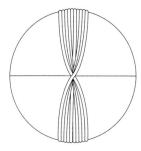

Wrapped bands with pivot point, page 71

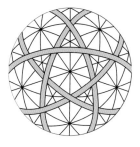

Weaving wrapped bands, page 74

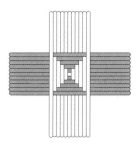

Inside to outside, page 72

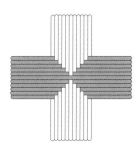

Outside to inside, page 72

Stitching Simple Shapes

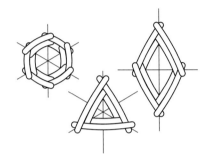

Open shapes, page 79

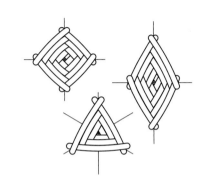

Solid shapes, page 84

Spindle, page 87

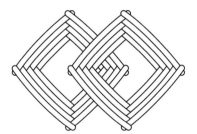

Overlapped stitching, page 89

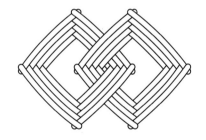

Interlocking stitching, page 89

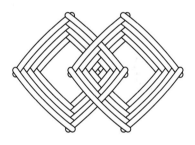

Layered stitching, page 92

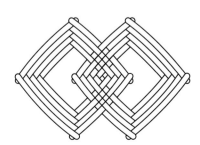

Weaving, page 89

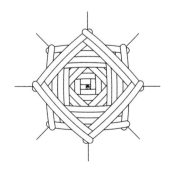

Rose design, page 133

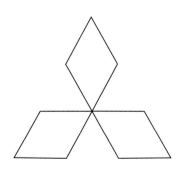

Mitsubishi **design (see three diamonds design), page 122**

Herringbone Stitches

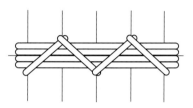

Single herringbone, page 95

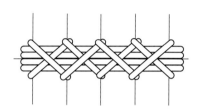

Double herringbone, page 95

Descending herringbone, page 106

Kiku herringbone, page 99

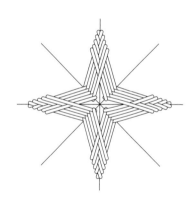

Reverse kiku herringbone, page 102

Ribbed kiku herringbone, page 105

Net stitching, page 97

Continuous Motifs

Solid five-point star, page 116

Open five-point star, interlocked, page 91

Open five-point star and pentagon, page 122

Solid tri-wing, layered, page 117

Interlocked tri-wing, page 118

Open tri-wing and hexagon, page 122

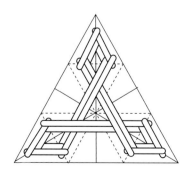

Interlocked continuous motif, page 118

Inward stitching on continuous motif, page 122

Continuous Motifs (continued)

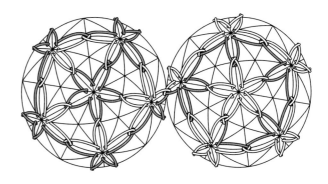

Hito hude gake (one stroke path), multiple motifs, page 124

Multiple motifs on C10, page 126

Merry-Go-Round

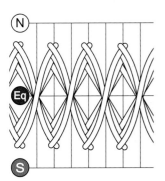

Merry-go-round design, page 109

Continuous Paths Stitching

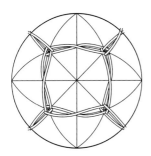

Continuous tri-wing, page 130

Paths through diamond shapes, page 131

Weaving

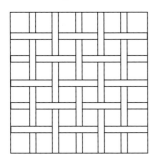

Box weaving, page 140

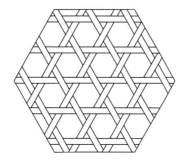

Hexagonal weave, page 141

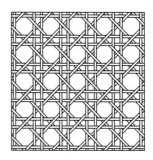

Octagonal weave, page 141

Flax Designs

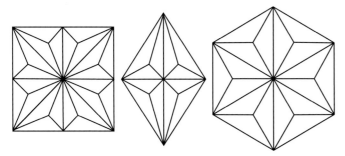

Flax leaf: individual motifs, page 145

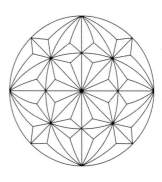

Flax design on C8, page 146

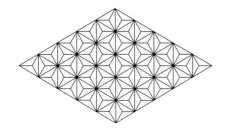

Flax leaf fill, page 149

V-Ruler

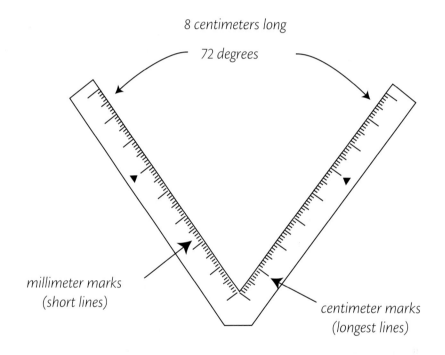

8 centimeters long

72 degrees

millimeter marks
(short lines)

centimeter marks
(longest lines)

V-ruler, page 41

Guide for Temari Teachers

Since temari making is a relatively unfamiliar craft outside of Japan, most of your students are likely to be beginners, who are the focus of this teaching plan. I have also included some guidance on working with more experienced temari enthusiasts. I hope you can use the guide as a starting point to create exciting classes of your own.

Choose a Place to Teach

Art centers, needlework shops, and craft stores are eager to hire teachers--especially for a class as unique as Japanese temari. Libraries and schools will happily make arrangements for you to donate your time by sharing your love for temari. They appreciate a hands-on class where the students make a temari or a simple grouping of your stitched temari to fill a display case. They will often provide supplies for students so you need only to give your time and skills. Embroiderers' Guild of America (EGA) or other textile art groups are often looking for programs for their meetings. Contact the groups to learn how to present proposals for classes.

You may find it best to hold practice classes in your home or church with family and friends first. Plan your lessons and then approach the store with a display of temari, a class outline, and a supply list for students. Make the display eye-catching (like a large jar full of balls) and provide written information on temari that prospective students can take home with them. Having a well-prepared class outline helps the store and the students know exactly what to expect as far as timing and techniques that will be covered. The supplies to make the temari should be purchased by the student at the store where you teach. This is a good way to give students options for different colors with their thread selection. You should be prepared to supply items not available in the store. If a student

Beginner's Kit

Ask the student to bring scissors that are small and sharp for cutting thread. They will need these items provided by the store or by you:

- One wrapped and marked ball (S8). Prepare this for them in advance for a very successful start!

- Darner needle with an eye large enough for perle cotton and a sharp point.

- Pins–a box of ball top pins in varying colors, about 1 ½"long.

- Core ingredients: either a Styrofoam ball or rice hulls with sock or stocking

- Yarn: 3 ounce skein of soft, baby yarn.

- Cone of serger thread: black is best for matching with any color stitching thread. You could supply three cones for power wrapping.

- Card or spool of metallic thread for guidelines.

- Stitching thread: perle cotton or craft thread.

has to bring only a pair of scissors, you know they will have all the right ingredients to have a successful start with the craft!

Lesson Plan for Beginning Stitchers

Beginners to the craft of temari need to have that first introductory class devoted just to them. You can give them all the instruction they need on making the ball and marking a simple division in a class that is all about beginning temari. Make it fun! Toss the balls around; bring yummy snacks. Prepare several designs and introduce new stitching skills with each one. Allot about two hours per design. Students probably won't finish the temari in two hours, but they will get a good start and understand how to complete it at home.

The timing for the class depends on the group. For classes held during the week, plan on scheduling two-or three-hour long classes over a period of several weeks. Students will be eager to complete their temari between classes and get feedback on the design learned in the previous class. An all-day Saturday class is great for people who work during the week. Follow the beginner's lesson plan, taking time for a lunch break and rest breaks during the day. You can fit three designs into a six hour class if you prepare two temari (wrapped and marked) to supply in the students' kits.

Class 1 As an introduction, talk about the history of temari and how you discovered the craft. Give a brief outline of the class and show the designs to be stitched. Bring temari from your collection for inspiration. Hand out the kits. Stitch Bermuda Reef (page 70). This easy, wrapped bands temari on an S8 division looks good in any combination of colors. While the students are stitching, demonstrate how to wrap balls with yarn and thread. Homework is to wrap a ball for the next class.

Class 2 Mark the ball that was wrapped at home into an S8 division. Have students choose two colors of thread for stitching and make Square Dance (page 83). They will learn to make the S8 division, stitch open squares, and stitch a double herringbone over the obi. Homework is to wrap a ball and mark in an S4 division.

Class 3 Check that all students were able to mark the ball at home and re-teach if necessary. Have students choose two colors of thread for stitching and make Lemon Slices (page 90). They will learn how to stitch spindles, a very important lesson in tension and placement of stitches, before moving on to the herringbone designs. Demonstrate how to mark an S6 division. Homework is to wrap a ball and mark in an S6 division.

Class 4 Check the marking done at home. Have students choose three colors of thread for stitching and make Daffodil (page 86). This fun design uses solid shapes and open shapes on the S6 division. Students learn to watch the sides and angles of the solid shapes to make sure they stay even.

Plans for Experienced Stitchers

Many basic techniques were covered in the first series of classes. Now that the student is able to prepare a wrapped and marked ball at home, the class will get off to a quick start by stitching the design right away. The class can be filled with students at the same level or you can offer a multi-level class. Work with students to select the pattern for each week and give them tips on how to prepare before coming to class. In a multi-level class, students will work on different patterns from the book and will be able to help each other by sharing experiences and tips on techniques. Listen to student feedback and requests to guide them through the large number of patterns in this book. At this point, you will probably not have to provide a kit; just let the students do their own shopping.

For a comprehensive study of temari, sequence the classes as below. When the basic technique is learned in class, discuss some of the endless variations that make temari so exciting to make!

1   Clematis Bloom (page 101): S12 division with kiku herringbone stitching

2   Classic Merry-Go-Round (page 111): learn the path around the ball with a basic herringbone stitch

3   Pearl Star (page 116): S10 division, solid 5-point star and open 5-point star

4   Pinwheel and Evening Star (pages 90 and 95): stitch one on each side of the same ball to compare interlocking with layering techniques

5   Mariposa Lily (page 119): tri-wing

6   Options for a C8 class: Three Diamonds (p 137), Raulston Roses (page 134), Flax Leaf All Around (page 147)

7   Options for a C10 class: Interlocked Puzzle (page 151), Emerald Isle (page 153)

8   Asters (page155): multi-centers marking

Index

14 faces, 47, 49
16 faces, 50-51
18 faces, 51
20 faces, 48-49

Abstracted Stars Pattern, 167
all-over design, 164-165
ami, see weaving
amime giku, see net stitching
Arai, Tomokazu, 8
asanoha kagari, see flax leaf
Asters Pattern, 155

basket temari, 75
bell box, 18-19
Bermuda Reef Pattern, 70
Blueberry Pie Pattern, 72
bin temari, 18
box weaving, 140
bundles, 71
Buttercups Pattern, 169

Caribbean Swirls Pattern, 67
chain stitch, 58
chidori kagari, see herringbone stitch
circle guide, 13
Classic *Hito Hude Gake* Pattern, 24, 127
Classic Kiku Pattern, 104
Classic Merry-Go-Round Pattern, 111
Clematis Bloom Pattern, 101
color, 106, 159-60
continuous motif, 115-127
    interlocked, 120
    inward stitching on, 122
continuous paths stitching, 129-130
    variations, 131
core, 17-21
    filling, 17-18

firm, 19
    materials, 17-18
    wrapping, 19-21
couching, 59
Country Night Pattern, 146
cross stitch, 58
curving, 82

Daffodil Pattern, 86
design, 157-165
    and color, 159-60
    elements of 157
    goal of, 158
    structure, 162-164
    visual unity of, 170
detached chain stitch, 59
diagram, 42
    combination division, 44-45
    simple division, 43
Diamond Dance Pattern, 129
display, 171-172
division, 29-41
    double C8, 32
    simple, 29, 31-32
    simple 4 (S4), 31-32
    combination, 29, 33-41
    combination 6 (C6), 34-35
    combination 8 (C8), 33-34
    combination 10 (C10), 36-41
Dusty Rose Pattern, 101

embroidery, 57-61
    chain stitch, 58
    couching, 59
    cross stitch, 58
    detached chain stitch, 59
    fly stitch, 60
    French knot, 57, 60

lazy daisy stitch, 59
Emerald Isle Pattern, 153
equator, 2
Evening Star Pattern, 93

Filigree Flax Pattern, 148
filling, 17-18
Five Diamonds *(Itsutsubishi)*
    Pattern, 138
five-point star, 115, 116
flax leaf, 145-149
fly stitch, 60
Forest Flower Pattern, 98
Four Diamonds *(Yotsubishi)*
    Pattern, 138
Four Tops Pattern, 166-167
French knot, 57, 60
Furosato no Temari, 8

guidelines, 25-55
    sharing, 164
    support, 46

herringbone, 95-107
    descending, 106
    double, 95-96
    kiku, 95, 96, 99
    reverse kiku, 102-103
    ribbed kiku, 105-106
    stitch, 95-97
hexagonal weaving, 143
hiding starts and stops, 75
hito hude gake, 117, 124-127, 129
    classic pattern, 127
hoshi kagari, see five-point star
Hot Pink Star Pattern, 123
hydrangea design, 94

Interlocked Puzzle Pattern, 151
interlocking shape, 89, 91
intersecting shape, 89
inward stitching, 122

Japan Temari Association, 7
Japanese terms, 2, 7, 9
Jasmine Pattern, 107
journal, 175

keeper pins, 71, 75, 110
kemari, 5
kiku herringbone, 99-101
    layering, 91, 124, 125
    stitch, 95, 99
kinsuke mari, 8
knot, 28
    display, 174

lazy daisy stitch, 59
layering, 91, 92
    wrapped bands, 72
Lemon Slices Pattern, 78, 88
Little Quilt Square Pattern, 77

maki kagari, 67
Mariposa Lily Pattern, 119
masu kagari, 79
materials, 13-15, 17
matsuba kagari, see pine needle stitching
measuring, 3
    by eye, 3
    strip, 12, 25-27, 67
Merry-Go-Round with Kiku
    Herringbone Pattern, 111
merry-go-round stitching, 109-113
mitusbane kikkou kagari, see tri-wing
mitsubishi, see three-diamond design

mitsume ami, see hexagonal weaving
multi-center, 53
    diamond-based, 55
    triangle-based, 54
Mums Pattern, 61

Nautical Mosaic Pattern, 73
needles, 12
needle-threading, 13
negative space, 169
nejiri kagari, see interlocking shape
net stitching, 97
north pole, 25-27
north-south concurrent stitching, 109

obi, 69
octagonal weaving, 141
one stroke of brush, see *hito hude gake*
onna-mari, 5
open shape, 79
overlapping, 89
Ozaki, Chiyoko, 6

paper measuring strip, 12, 25-27, 67
pattern,
    Abstracted Stars, 167
    Asters, 155
    Bermuda Reef, 70
    Blueberry Pie, 72
    Buttercups, 169
    Caribbean Swirls, 67
    Classic *Hito Hude Gake*, 24, 127
    Classic Kiku, 104
    Classic Merry-Go-Round, 111
    Clematis Bloom, 101
    Country Night, 146
    Daffodil, 86
    Diamond Dance, 129

    Dusty Rose, 101
    Emerald Isle, 153
    Evening Star, 93
    Filigree Flax, 148
    Five Diamonds *(Itsutsubishi)*, 138
    Forest Flower, 98
    Four Diamonds *(Yotsubishi)*, 138, 167
    Four Tops, 167
    Hot Pink Star, 123
    Interlocked Puzzle, 151
    Jasmine, 107
    Lemon Slices, 78, 88
    Little Quilt Square, 77
    Mariposa Lily, 119
    Merry-Go-Round with Kiku
        Herringbone, 111
    Mums, 61
    Nautical Mosaic, 73
    Pearl Star, 116
    Pinwheel, 90
    Raulston Roses, 134
    Red Dahlia, 104
    Square Dance, 83
    Summer Picnic Basket, 77
    Three Diamonds *(Mitusbishi)*, 137
    Weave Study, 143
    Whirly Bird, 121
    Woven Bamboo, 143
Pearl Star Pattern, 116
pillow, 13, 172
pine needle stitching, 63
pins, 12, 27
Pinwheel Pattern, 90
pivot point, 71, 109-110
pole-to-pole stitching, 109

Raulston Roses Pattern, 132, 134
recycling, 9

Red Dahlia Pattern, 104
renzoku kagari, see continuous paths
    stitching
restart, 82
reverse kiku herringbone, 102-103
ribbed kiku herringbone, 105-106
rose design, 133-134

sakasa kagari, see inward stitching
scissors, 12
shishu, 57
shitagake chidori kagari, see descending
    herringbone
simple division, 29, 31-32
solid shape, 84
south pole, 26-27
spacing, 81, 87
spindle, 87
Square Dance Pattern, 83
square weaving, 140
stained glass effects, 135
stitch, 81
    choice of, 162
    order, 93
stop, 82
structure, 162-163
subdividing guidelines, 46-55
    14 faces, 47, 49
    16 faces, 50-51
    18 faces, 51
    20 faces, 48-49
    C8 division, 49-51

C10 division, 53-55
single shape, 46
    multiple shapes with continuous
        path, 46
    multi-centers, 53
sujidagiku kagari, see ribbed kiku
    herringbone
Summer Picnic Basket Pattern, 77
support guidelines, 25-55
surface embroidery, see embroidery
swirl stitching, 65
symbolism, 160-161
symmetry, 74, 170

tacking intersections, 30
tape measure, 13
tassel, 173-174
teenie temari, 23
temari uta, 6
Temari Juni Kagetsu, 6
Temari no Kai, see Japan Temari
Association
tension, 19-20, 70, 87
texture, 15
thimble, 13
thread,
    ending off, 29
    hanger, 173
    length, 67
    overlap, 82
    starting, 27-28
    types, 13-15

three-diamond design, 135
Three Diamonds *(Mitsubishi)* Pattern,
    137
tools, 11-13
trefoil, 117
tri-axial shape, 141
tri-wing, 115, 117
    continuous, 130

vintage temari, 6-7
v-ruler, 13, 41

Weave Study Pattern, 142
weaving, 89, 139-143
Woven Bamboo Pattern, 143
wrapped band,
    basic, 67-69
    layering, 72
    symmetry, 74
wrapping, 67-77
    along guidelines, 70
    core, 19-21
    pivot point, 71
    tension, 70
    yarn, 20
Whirly Bird Pattern, 121
Woven Bamboo Pattern, 143
yatsume ami, see octagonal weaving

zabuton, 172

If You Enjoyed Temari Techniques, You'll Love *Japanese Temari* by Barbara B. Suess

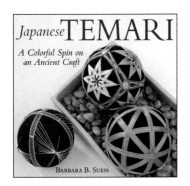

How can anything that looks so intricate be so simple! Try it out and see! With nothing more than a needle and thread, Barbara B. Suess shows you how to make beautiful Japanese temari balls in dozens of colors and patterns. Perfect for stitching on the go, the balls make beautiful gifts and are wonderful home-dec accessories. Requiring few materials and just a little practice, *Japanese Temari* offers 26 designs to choose from. At every step, there are color drawings that show you exactly what to do, as well as gorgeous photos to inspire you. Each pattern introduces as new skill, helping you build your temari repertoire as you stitch your way through the book. Lovely watercolor drawings, haiku poetry, and insights into Japan's artistic traditions make this book a delight to browse as you plan your next temari project.

ISBN: 978-1933308-12-8 $24.95

And for Another Unique Japanese Craft, Try *Japanese Kimekomi* by Barbara B. Suess and Kathy M. Hewitt

Are you in search of a fast, easy, and oh-so fun new craft to amaze your friends and family? How about one with a unique Japanese spin? Welcome to the world of kimekomi—amazing Japanese fabric handballs, created in every pattern and color you can imagine. Unbelievably simple to make, each one makes a delightful and unusual gift. Make them as Christmas ornaments, Easter gifts, home-dec accessories—or as lightweight handballs for your favorite child. Even your first ball will be complete in a couple of hours, and you need no more than a Styrofoam ball, a handful of colored fabric scraps, a little glue, and pretty ribbons or cords for embellishment.

* 15 bright, colorful designs--including one in the shape of a traditional Easter egg!

* Color step-by-step drawings, sensational photos, and easy-to-follow text

* Full size cutting templates for every design

* Beyond the basics—a special section on creating new designs of your own

ISBN: 978-19333082-1-0 $19.95

For more information on both books, visit our website at www.brecklingpress.com